Buried in Treasures

Buried in Treasures

*Help for Compulsive Acquiring,
Saving, and Hoarding*

SECOND EDITION

David F. Tolin • Randy O. Frost • Gail Steketee

OXFORD
UNIVERSITY PRESS

OXFORD

UNIVERSITY PRESS

Oxford University Press is a department of the University of Oxford.
It furthers the University's objective of excellence in research, scholarship,
and education by publishing worldwide.

Oxford   New York
Auckland   Cape Town   Dar es Salaam   Hong Kong   Karachi
Kuala Lumpur   Madrid   Melbourne   Mexico City   Nairobi
New Delhi   Shanghai   Taipei   Toronto

With offices in
Argentina   Austria   Brazil   Chile   Czech Republic   France   Greece
Guatemala   Hungary   Italy   Japan   Poland   Portugal   Singapore
South Korea   Switzerland   Thailand   Turkey   Ukraine   Vietnam

Published in the United States of America by
Oxford University Press
198 Madison Avenue, New York, NY 10016

Library of Congress Cataloging-in-Publication Data
Tolin, David F.
Buried in treasures: help for compulsive acquiring, saving,
and hoarding / David F. Tolin,
Randy O. Frost, Gail Steketee. — Second edition.
    pages cm. — (Treatments that work)
Includes index.
ISBN 978–0–19–932925–0
1. Obsessive-compulsive disorder.   2. Compulsive hoarding.
I.   Frost, Randy O. II.   Steketee, Gail.
III.   Title.
RC533.T65 2014
616.85′227—dc23
2013028718

9 8 7
Printed in the United States of America
on acid-free paper

Acknowledgments

David thanks his wife, Fiona, and their kids, James and Katie, for their support.

Randy would like to thank his wife, Sue, for her support and encouragement.

Gail thanks her husband, Brian McCorkle, for his patience and thoughtful contributions to her research and clinical work on hoarding.

All of us extend our thanks to the many people whose lives are afflicted by hoarding and who have helped us learn about this challenging problem in our clinics and research centers. This book is dedicated to all of you.

Contents

Buried in Treasures

Introduction

✳ About This Book

This book is for and about people who have trouble managing their possessions. When we published the first edition of *Buried in Treasures* in 2007, not many people had heard of hoarding. Even doctors and health-care professionals had little or no understanding of this phenomenon, even though it was (and remains) very common. Things have certainly changed since then! Hoarding has been featured on such popular television programs as *The Oprah Winfrey Show* and *The Dr. Oz Show*. Entire TV series, such as *Hoarders* (A&E), *Hoarders: Buried Alive* (TLC), and *Confessions: Animal Hoarding* (Animal Planet), have been dedicated to the topic. These media portrayals have their strengths and weaknesses, but there's no denying the fact that they have brought hoarding into the national spotlight. Hoarding has gone from being virtually unheard of to a household word.

Changes have also occurred outside the popular media. The most recent edition of the *Diagnostic and Statistical Manual of Mental Disorders* (DSM-5), published by the American Psychiatric Association in 2013, now includes for the first time a diagnosis of "Hoarding Disorder." That's what this book is about—Hoarding Disorder. We've written it mainly for people who are suffering from hoarding, although we also hope it is useful for people whose loved ones hoard, and professionals who work with people who hoard. Our aim in writing this book is to provide you with clear, up-to-date information about hoarding, and to provide you with a plan to gain control over your hoarding problems, whether they are mild or severe.

Now, let's start by saying that not everyone likes the word "hoarding." For many, terms like "excessive saving, acquiring, and clutter" sound a bit less offensive (and they are certainly more descriptive). And there's no doubt that a lot of people don't like the word "hoarder." Some prefer terms like "pack rat" or "clutterbug," but in the end, people are more than a label, even if the label seems less offensive. We therefore avoid the term "hoarder" in this book and instead refer to "people with hoarding problems" or similar terms. We have retained the term "hoarding," mostly because "excessive saving, acquiring, and clutter" is just too cumbersome. We hope you will understand that this is shorthand, and not meant as name-calling.

We'll start by describing the problem in Chapter 2 and introducing you to a couple of people who hoard. Their problems may seem familiar to you, or maybe your situation is a bit different. In any case, we hope you will take away some of the basic principles and have a better understanding of the hoarding problem. In Chapters 2 and 6, we discuss how hoarding develops and why people have such a hard time overcoming this problem. The rest of the book is dedicated to providing you with a step-by-step plan for getting control over hoarding thinking, emotions, and behavior. After an overview of all the strategies in Chapter 5, we'll work on keeping your motivation high in Chapter 7, help you reduce acquiring things that add to the clutter in Chapter 8, show you how to sort and let go of possessions in Chapters 9 and 10, describe how to tackle problems that come up in Chapters 11 and 12, and discuss ways to maintain your gains in the long run in Chapter 13.

Sounds pretty good, right? At this point, we should probably caution you: *Just reading this book will not solve your hoarding problems.* If that's all you do, nothing will change. We realize that saying this in the first pages of our book might be disappointing, but it's important that we be honest and that you understand what this book can and cannot do for you. This book is a guide that will provide you with the necessary information to understand the problem of hoarding and will give you tools to help beat the problem. The rest is up to you. You are the one who will have to do the work to regain control over your possessions. *This book is a roadmap. You are the driver.*

Getting control of your hoarding will be hard work. We have never met anyone who found this process easy. For most people, it took a long time for the problem to build up to its present level, and it's not going to get better overnight. In addition, it might not always be a pleasant process. We think you will find the overall program to be very rewarding, and we hope that you get a lot of satisfaction from the results. However, there may be times that this program brings up some uncomfortable feelings and thoughts that perhaps you'd rather not experience. There may even be times that you want to throw this book out the window! But that's a very normal part of the process, and it's OK to have mixed feelings as you go through this. If you are willing to work hard, to keep your eyes on your goals, and to follow the program in this book, you can do it.

Another thing to keep in mind is that your goal is to change the way you think about the things you own and the decisions you make about them. Decluttering your home will be part of the program, but changing the way you relate to possessions is what will make this approach successful. This means making some changes in your lifestyle that will continue long after you finish with this book. This book is designed to get you started on that journey.

Finally, it's important to remember that *one size doesn't fit all*. People acquire and save for many reasons, so they will need to try different methods in order to get better. In addition, some people reading this book will have only mild hoarding problems, while others' problems might be quite severe and debilitating. There's no way we could write a book that will be a perfect fit for everyone. If only the solution were as simple as handing you a couple of exercises and guaranteeing they will work! But of course, it is not that simple.

In this book we've tried to provide a framework to help you understand and work on hoarding the way we do—flexibly, trying different things and modifying the program as you go. So as you use this book, there might be some parts that just don't apply to you. That's fine; just skim those parts for reference if you like. But pay special attention to those parts of the book that seem to fit what you're noticing in your own life, and work especially hard on those exercises.

✳ Who Should Use This Book and How?

We have designed the information in this book to be applicable to a wide range of people who are concerned about hoarding. We recognize that if you're like most of the people with hoarding problems we've met, you didn't choose to have this problem and are very unhappy with how things are going. You want things to get better but just don't know where or how to start.

To begin with, congratulations are in order. Your purchase of this book is the first step toward beating this problem, and that's no small feat. A lot of people never make it as far as you have now. Perhaps, however, this is not the first book you've bought on the subject. We've met a lot of people whose purchase of books about how to declutter and get organized just added to their clutter! We would like nothing more than for this to be the last book you ever buy on this topic. What's different about this book? Unlike many of the other books you may have seen, the information in this book is based on the best available science. Although we still have a long way to go before we have a complete understanding of hoarding, the strategies in this book have been "road tested" in our research programs sponsored by the National Institutes of Health. As we write this book, research on understanding and fixing hoarding is ongoing. The great news is that the majority of people who have participated in our clinical research in Boston, Hartford, and Northampton have shown significant improvement. The tips and strategies in this book reflect what we've found successful for the people who come to see us.

While you can certainly use this book on your own, in the last few years, a number of people have begun to use the chapters of *Buried in Treasures* together in small groups. These Buried in Treasures (BIT) Workshops are going on across the country now, and they have proven nearly as successful as individual therapy for hoarding using very similar methods. If you know of or would like to find other people who need help with this problem, we encourage you to consider forming a BIT Workshop. The BIT Workshop method is highly structured, with each session focusing on a chapter from this book and everyone working through the exercises in it. There is no professional therapist, just someone who takes on the role of facilitator. Everything you need to know to run one of these workshops can be found in a facilitator's guide that is available for free at the International OCD Foundation Web site (www. ocfoundation.org/hoarding). The guide is called *Leading the Buried in Treasures Workshop: A Facilitator's Manual* and is written for people with hoarding problems.

If you are a family member or friend of someone who has a hoarding problem, this book is for you too. We hear from a lot of people like you, and we know how difficult it is to watch a family member or friend go through this and how frustrating it is not to be able to do anything about it. We've lost track of how many people—hundreds, maybe thousands—have contacted us with questions like, "My mother (father, daughter, brother, etc.) has mountains of clutter but doesn't acknowledge that anything's wrong. The whole family has talked to him/her about it, but the conversation always turns into an argument. How can I convince him/her to do something about it?" It's great that you want to help, and we will try to help you. In various places, you'll notice breakout boxes with the title "Fact File for Family and Friends." These boxes contain information specially designed for you.

Still other people reading this book will be mental health professionals, social service workers, or professional organizers who work with people with hoarding problems. For many of you, hoarding has represented a special challenge in your practice. We get questions like, "I've been treating someone for depression for a long time, and I never knew he/she had a hoarding problem until his/her relative contacted me. Why didn't my client tell me about it?" Or, "Our agency has been getting complaints about clutter outside someone's home—but the person seems reluctant to do much about it, no matter how much we talk to him/her." We hope this book will give you some insight into what we know about hoarding and how we go about treating it in our clinics. If you're a mental health professional, you will probably find the therapist guide (see breakout box) useful, as it provides strategies for cognitive-behavioral therapy that are not included here.

The specific things to look for and the way to use this book will vary somewhat depending on who you are. If you are a person with a hoarding problem (and in the coming chapters we'll help you find out whether you are), you have a couple of options. The first option is to use this book as a standalone program for beating hoarding. This is perfectly fine and makes sense as a first shot. But, if that does not work well enough, consider forming or joining a Buried in Treasures Workshop. One of the participants in a recent BIT Workshop made the following comment about it: "I first read the book and revved up my uncluttering. But when I re-read the book with my support group and did all the exercises, I understood myself better. I didn't just clear out some space. I changed." This is the kind of outcome you can achieve if you keep at it.

Another thing to consider is to use this book in addition to seeing a professional mental health worker such as a psychologist, social worker, psychiatrist, or psychiatric nurse. Two of the authors of this book (Gail Steketee and Randy

Frost) have written a manual for clinicians and an accompanying client workbook that follows the same program as this book (see breakout box). You can suggest that the professional follow along with his/her own manual. If you decide you would like help from a professional while you go through this program, good resources for finding a therapist are the International OCD Foundation (www.ocfoundation.org/treatment_providers) and the Association of Behavioral and Cognitive Therapists (www.abct.org, click on "Find a Therapist").

Treatments *ThatWork*™

Treatment for Hoarding Disorder, Therapist Guide, Second Edition

Treatment for Hoarding Disorder, Workbook, Second Edition

By Gail Steketee and Randy O. Frost
Oxford University Press

✳ "Ugh, how am I supposed to digest an entire book?"

We realize that it can be quite daunting to start a self-help program. And if you're like a lot of people with hoarding problems, you might find that it's hard to sustain attention and focus for a long time (more on that later). Don't worry. We've done our best to make this as straightforward as possible. First, we have tried not to clutter up the book with scientific jargon, statistics, citations, and so on. Even though this book is based on scientific research, we've deliberately kept a lot of details out so the book will be easy to read for people without a background in science. Second, you might notice that we repeat ourselves from time to time. That's deliberate. We know from decades of research that people learn best when they read something more than once—and that's especially true for people who have problems of attention. So don't worry about trying to memorize everything in the book—we've made sure that you'll get the important points more than once, in a variety of contexts.

✳ "Are you guys going to make me throw out all of my cherished possessions?"

No. First of all, we're not going to make you do anything—we couldn't even if we wanted to. We believe firmly in respecting people's autonomy and control. Your possessions belong to you, and only you can decide what to do with them. Second, although it's easy to focus on discarding (indeed, on the hoarding-related TV shows a lot of emphasis is placed on throwing stuff out), we think that this is only part of the picture. When your home is filled to the brim with stuff, it's hard to get any enjoyment out of your possessions. The good stuff might well be buried underneath a pile of other stuff, so it's hard to find. Even if you do find the good stuff, you might not have enough room to enjoy it. Or you might find that after being buried under a pile for a long time, the good stuff has deteriorated to the point where it's not so good anymore. The critical issue, then, is to *make room in your home for the things you value most*. A major goal of this book is to enable you to celebrate and enjoy the things you save. This program will help.

When Is It Time to Seek Professional Help?

There's no hard-and-fast rule here. Seeking professional help is a very personal decision, and different people have different criteria for making that decision. Our criteria (which might differ from yours) are that you should consider consulting a professional (a) if the problem seems too overwhelming to manage on your own or with the help of friends or family; (b) if the strategies in this book don't seem to help; or (c) if other mental health concerns such as anxiety or depression seem to be getting in the way of beating the hoarding problem. Below, we'll describe some of the different kinds of treatment and the types of people who can provide them.

Therapy

Traditional "talk therapy" doesn't seem to be particularly helpful for people with hoarding problems. We do have evidence, however, that a particular kind of psychological therapy—cognitive-behavioral therapy (CBT)—is helpful for people with hoarding. What's unique about CBT? Unlike other kinds of therapy or counseling, CBT is a very active solution-focused treatment in which you and the therapist work together to learn how to sort and let go of possessions, think more clearly about your possessions, and control the urges

How to find a therapist:

American Psychological
    Association
Web site: http://www.apa.org/
Telephone: 800-374-2721;
202-336-5500

Anxiety Disorders Association
    of America
Web site: http://www.adaa.org/
Telephone: 240-485-1001

Association of Behavioral and
    Cognitive Therapies
Web site: http://www.aabt.org/
Telephone: 212-647-1890

Council on Social Work Education
Web site: http://www.cswe.org/
Telephone: 703-683-8080

National Association of Social
    Workers
Web site: http://www.naswdc.org/
Telephone: 202-408-8600

International OCD Foundation
Web site: http://www.ocfounda-
    tion.org/
Telephone: 203-401-2070

to acquire. In our clinics and research studies, the therapist even goes to the person's home to help him or her learn how it's done. We have been studying the effects of CBT for people with hoarding, and our evidence shows that the majority of people who go through this treatment show substantial improvement in the level of clutter and in how they feel. What we have also found is that in most cases, the person's condition improved and he or she was happy with the results but still had more clutter than the average person and had to continue to work at it. CBT is usually provided by a psychologist or social worker, although not all psychologists and social workers practice this kind of treatment.

When selecting a therapist, it is important to find out whether he or she is an expert in CBT and has experience treating hoarding. Unfortunately, most clinicians are not yet very experienced at treating hoarding problems, but if the person is skilled at CBT and reads this book and/or Steketee and Frost's treatment manual, this will go a long way toward enabling him or her to help. At this time, the best places to find a therapist who knows how to treat hoarding are the International OCD Foundation Web site (www.ocfoundation.org) and the Association for Behavioral and Cognitive Therapies Web site (www.abct. org), both of which contain interactive pages for finding a therapist in your area.

Medications

So far, very little research has examined the use of medication to treat hoarding. Medications used to treat obsessive-compulsive disorder (OCD) have

American Psychiatric Association
Web site: http://www.psych.org/
Telephone: 703-907-7300
E-mail: apa@psych.org

also been used for hoarding. These medications include serotonin reuptake inhibitors (SRI) such as clomipramine, as well as selective serotonin reuptake inhibitors (SSRI) such as fluvoxamine, fluoxetine, sertraline, and paroxetine. Some new evidence suggests that some of the SSRIs (especially paroxetine and venlafaxine) may be helpful for hoarding, but other evidence indicates that these medications are not as useful for treating hoarding as they are for OCD. Legally, any physician can prescribe medications. However, we generally recommend that you consult a psychiatrist or advanced practice nurse who has special expertise in prescribing psychiatric medications.

Professional Organizers

It's important to remember that serious mental health problems require treatment from a trained mental health professional. However, we think that professional organizers can be a very useful addition to your team. Professional organizers have a term called "chronic disorganization," which is similar in many ways to our concept of hoarding. The subgroup of professional organizers who specialize in dealing with this kind of problem is called the Institute for Challenging Disorganization. Professional organizers, particularly those with this specialty, are great at helping you figure out ways to organize and manage the possessions in your home. In fact, some of what we do in treatment is borrowed from the work of professional organizers.

The concept of "chronic disorganization," used by professional organizers, is similar in many ways to hoarding. The Institute for Challenging Disorganization (ICD) has outlined the following characteristics as signs of chronic disorganization:

- Accumulation of large quantities of objects, documents, papers, or possessions beyond apparent necessity or pleasure

- Difficulty parting with things and letting go

- A wide range of interests and many uncompleted projects

- Need for visual "clues" to remind one to take action

- Tendency to be easily distracted or lose concentration

- Poor time-management skills

For more information, visit the ICD Web site at www.challengingdisorganization.org.

Stepped Care

Increasingly, doctors and researchers have been interested in a concept called *stepped care*. That means that you can start with one treatment—usually something relatively easy and inexpensive—and then move up to more intensive treatments only if they are needed. For many people, this is a very sensible way to work on a problem—try something simple first, see if that works, and if it doesn't, do something more complicated. This book can be a great first step in a stepped care program. We know from our experience that it will help some people, perhaps even most people, but it won't help everyone. So here's a way to think about your own stepped care program:

1. Try this program, on your own or with the help of a friend or family member. Pay careful attention to what works and what doesn't work for you.

2. If it seems like this program has adequately addressed the hoarding problem, great! Keep it up and congratulate yourself. If not, consider finding or forming a BIT Workshop. Our experience has shown that a BIT Workshop can be beneficial even after trying to use this book on your own.

3. If, after you've given this a good try (meaning you really did your best with it and kept up with it for a reasonable amount of time), the hoarding problem still hasn't gotten better, don't despair. It just means that you probably need to take the next step, which would be consulting with a professional. But even in that case, this book can lay the groundwork for future success with a therapist or organizer.

✳ What's New in the Second Edition of *Buried in Treasures?*

Our understanding of hoarding, and our ability to do something about it, is constantly evolving. As we mentioned previously, since we published the first edition of *Buried in Treasures*, there's been an astonishing explosion of public and scientific interest in the topic of hoarding. First, the new edition of the *Diagnostic and Statistical Manual of Mental Disorders* includes, for the first time, the diagnosis of Hoarding Disorder; we have incorporated those diagnostic criteria here (see Chapter 2). We've interviewed readers who attended our Buried in Treasures Workshops and found out what they found more or less easy to digest; we have tried to be clearer about those areas they told us were confusing. We also have provided more information about the findings of our clinical trials that show what works with hoarding and where we still have room for improvement. We've improved our self-assessment tools (see Chapter 3) to help you prioritize safety and to conduct your own experiments to help you understand why you save things. As we've learned more about what stops people from overcoming hoarding—we call these the "bad guys"—we've added more emphasis on psychological issues such as perfectionism, stress, and time-management problems (see Chapter 4). We've also added a new strategy to our "good guys" on setting manageable goals and gradually increasing your stamina. In Chapter 6, we update you on the latest research (ours and others') about how hoarding is related to brain function. These changes are designed to keep you up to date with the best available information about hoarding and to keep you on track with the best possible strategies for beating it. We hope you find these revisions helpful.

2

What Is Hoarding?

Over the past 50 years, the number of possessions owned by the average person has increased dramatically. Modern civilizations are based on consumerism, saving, and acquiring; the more people accumulate, the better the country does from an economic standpoint. For most of us, it is not particularly difficult to manage our possessions—in fact, most people find it pleasurable. We buy what we need (although sometimes we may overdo it), and we discard, recycle, donate, or sell what we don't need. We also tend to modify the amount of stuff we own to accommodate the available living space: people living in grand homes tend to buy and save more things than do people living in studio apartments. If our living space starts to feel cluttered or uncomfortable, we remove objects until our homes are the way we like them.

Some of us, however, have much more trouble resisting acquiring, and we save too many possessions. We save and save until the clutter starts to create problems in living. Family members or friends might start to comment on how messy our homes are, or even argue with us about this. We might agree with them, or we might not—but even if we do want to make a change, we don't know where to start. We feel overwhelmed and intimidated by the idea of getting rid of things. In short, our possessions own *us* rather than the other way around.

Does this sound like you? If so, you might be suffering from a condition known as *Hoarding Disorder.* The most recent edition of the *Diagnostic and Statistical Manual of Mental Disorders* (DSM-5), published by the American

Psychiatric Association, states that Hoarding Disorder is present when the following criteria are met:

1. Persistent difficulty discarding or parting with possessions, regardless of their actual value.

2. This difficulty is due to a perceived need to save the items and distress associated with discarding them.

It's hard for people with Hoarding Disorder to discard, donate, recycle, or otherwise "let go" of their possessions. For them, the possessions take on special meaning. For some people, the item represents a potential opportunity they just can't pass up. For others, the item feels like an old friend they don't want to part with. Some people find it difficult to throw away things that seem pretty or nice. Still others worry that discarding items would be wasteful. Sometimes parting with possessions is possible, but the process is so elaborate, time-consuming, and unpleasant that the home fills up. By this point, the items have overstayed their welcome—but when the time comes to make a decision, the person feels overwhelmed and the urge to save outweighs the urge to purge.

The definition of hoarding further specifies that items are saved "regardless of their actual value." This is an important point. Until recently, psychiatrists and psychologists erroneously believed that hoarding involved only the inability to discard "worthless and worn-out" things. Our research has discovered that this is not true. People with hoarding problems have difficulty letting go of most possessions, *regardless of their actual value*. Many of the people we study have closets full of clothes with the tags still on, or never-used appliances still in their original packaging. While it is true that people with hoarding problems often see value in things that other people don't, the real problem is the volume of possessions and how they are organized, not their actual value.

The third criterion for Hoarding Disorder is:

3. The symptoms result in the accumulation of possessions that congest and clutter active living areas and substantially compromise their intended use.

Many people are messy. In fact, most people's homes have at least some degree of clutter—things that they don't particularly want or need but for one reason or another haven't gotten rid of or straightened up. We don't know very many people who are 100 percent satisfied with the neatness or cleanliness of their home (we certainly aren't). The important distinction, however, is that most "messy" people typically can use their home in the way they originally intended. In contrast, people with hoarding frequently tell us that their clutter prevents them from using part or all of their homes. For example, many people say that they can't cook or eat in their kitchens because clutter has taken over the sink, stovetop, and kitchen table. They can't relax or invite guests into their living room, because the clutter has taken over the furniture and the floor. Others tell us that they can't sleep in their bed because clothing is piled all over it. In some cases, clutter has even found its way into the bathtub or shower, preventing the person from bathing. These living areas have been converted into makeshift storage areas, and the house has become, in the words of comedian George Carlin, "just a pile of stuff with a cover on it."

The fourth criterion for Hoarding Disorder is:

4. The hoarding causes clinically significant distress or impairment in social, occupational, or other important areas of functioning.

As we have described above, one of the key features of hoarding is that the clutter is so bad that portions of the home are difficult to use for anything other than storage. It's not hard to imagine that the person's quality of life often suffers dramatically. If you cannot cook, eat, sleep, or even walk through the house without tremendous difficulty, it's hard to feel anything but unhappy. This is what separates hoarding from collecting and other behaviors in which people accumulate large quantities of material possessions. The number of possessions is less important in defining hoarding than how much the resulting clutter interferes with the ability to live comfortably. Hoarding can also be a dangerous problem, putting people at substantial risk for fire, falling, respiratory problems, and other health risks. This may be particularly true for older people who already have difficulty walking and could be injured badly if they fell.

> *One of the key features of hoarding is that the clutter is so bad that portions of the home are difficult to use.*

Those are the main criteria for Hoarding Disorder: difficulty discarding, strong urges to save things, clutter, and distress or impaired functioning.

In addition, the DSM lists two "specifiers" (features that may or may not be present):

1. *Excessive acquiring:* People who hoard often can't stop themselves from acquiring things no matter how hard they try. In some cases, they buy more than they need at stores, yard sales, or flea markets. In other cases, they acquire free things such as extra newspapers, advertisements, or discarded items from street trash or dumpsters. A few people with hoarding have even resorted to stealing to satisfy their urge to accumulate things. Accumulating objects is sometimes a form of "retail therapy" in which the buying and acquiring soothes a negative mood or distracts the person from uncomfortable thoughts. Although some people get a good deal of joy and fulfillment from buying things they like or finding "good deals," it is a problem when the person doesn't have enough money and space in the home to keep pace with the number of objects acquired.

> People who hoard often can't stop themselves from acquiring things no matter how hard they try.

2. *Poor insight:* Some, but certainly not all, people with Hoarding Disorder have difficulty grasping the severity of their problem. They genuinely wonder why everyone else is making such a fuss about it. As a result, they often resist attempts by others to intervene, even when the clutter has become hazardous. This lack of awareness of the severity of the hoarding problem can be especially frustrating to family members and friends who want to help.

> Take-home message:
> Hoarding is a problem that involves difficulty discarding a large number of things, regardless of their actual value. We consider the problem to be serious when it prevents you from using your living spaces effectively and causes significant distress or affects your ability to function.

✳ How Bad Is the Problem?

Hoarding can range from mild to life-threatening. To help illustrate different hoarding situations, we'd like to introduce you to a couple of people who share this problem. Although these people are fictitious, their experiences are based on those of several people we have met and worked with in our clinics and research studies.

✳ *Helen is a 55-year-old woman who describes herself as having always been a pack rat. She tends to save things just in case she'll need them later, and she has always had a tendency to let these things pile up in her home. However, she indicates that the condition of her home got significantly worse after her divorce 8 years ago. Now she has difficulty throwing almost anything away. When junk mail, like credit card advertisements and charity solicitations, comes into her home, she doesn't throw them away because she's afraid they might be important. She keeps meaning to open the envelopes and find out what's inside, but the more the pile has grown, the more overwhelmed she feels. Now, when she looks at the clutter, she feels extremely sad and fatigued and doesn't feel up to dealing with it. When her adult daughter last came to visit, she found it difficult to walk through the house, as she navigated around precarious piles of paper, clothing, containers, and other items. Helen had also been adding to the problem over the past several years due to her difficulty resisting sales. When she saw a good bargain—for example, deep discounts on clothing—she felt she would be missing out on a great opportunity if she didn't buy something. In reality, she never actually wore many of the clothes she purchased, and often left them crumpled in a pile in her bedroom.*

✳ *Bill, a 40-year-old man, was referred to our clinic by his town's social service agency after they received numerous complaints from neighbors about the condition of Bill's property. The exterior of his house was in disrepair, and old, rusting cars and nonworking appliances littered his yard. Bill told us, "I'm always on the lookout for a good deal." He spent most of his free time visiting flea markets, discount stores, and junkyards looking for bargains. His plan was to fix up these items and then either give them as gifts to his family or sell them for profit. However, in the 20 years he had been acquiring items, he couldn't recall having sold anything, and he had given very few gifts. Instead, the items he acquired were thrown on top of giant piles in his home. When the therapist first visited Bill's house, she had to squeeze through the side door, which was partially blocked by old furniture; all of the other entrances to the house were completely blocked and unusable. Items were piled nearly floor to ceiling throughout the house, and Bill was able to walk through parts of his home only on narrow paths through the clutter. Some rooms were completely blocked off by a wall of clutter. The house smelled like rotting food, and insects buzzed around. Many of the appliances, such as the stove and refrigerator, no longer worked, having broken years ago, and the home was too cluttered to permit access by repairmen.*

Helen and Bill both have the same basic problem, hoarding, but it is expressed in very different ways. Helen's problem is milder at this stage of her life, whereas Bill's is severe. Helen's hoarding behavior is mostly characterized by difficulty getting rid of things for fear she will need them later, whereas Bill's behavior is focused on excessive acquiring due to unrealistic beliefs about how he will use the items he acquires. We will come back to Helen and Bill to help illustrate aspects of hoarding and how to work on the problem throughout this book.

✳ What Is the Natural Course of Hoarding?

We surveyed a large number of adults with hoarding problems. We were surprised to find that most of them reported that they first noticed hoarding-related behaviors very early in their lives, during childhood or early adolescence. For example, some recalled being "savers" or "collectors" early on. Sometimes they started hoarding after a bad or traumatic experience. One woman began to barricade the upstairs bedroom in which she had been assaulted and gradually kept adding clutter to the hallway, the next room, and other parts of her home. In other cases, however, there was no clear trigger for the behavior. In most cases, they did not develop a substantial clutter problem until they were adults, due in part to the fact that their parents helped control the problem while they were living with them.

Researchers at Johns Hopkins University have shown that hoarding runs in families. Many people tell us that they had one or more relatives (parent, sibling, aunt or uncle, grandparent) who were pack rats or had difficulty getting rid of things. Some scientific evidence suggests that there may be a genetic component to hoarding. Does this mean that hoarding is inherited, and nothing can

Some scientific evidence suggests that there may be a genetic component to hoarding.

be done about it? Certainly not. First, it's very unlikely that anyone inherits hoarding behaviors in the way that he or she would inherit, say, eye color. Rather, people may inherit a set of brain characteristics or temperamental features that make it *easier* for them to develop hoarding problems under the right circumstances—but that's not the same thing as inheriting hoarding itself. Second, it is important to remember that biology is not destiny. Regardless of the physical or genetic qualities of hoarding, you can learn to overcome it.

Several large community surveys have been conducted to estimate how many people actually have Hoarding Disorder. When we first saw the results, we were flabbergasted: the rate of hoarding may be as high as 5 percent, or 1 out of every 20 people! That's over 15 million people in the United States, over 25 million people in the European Union, and over 348 million people in the world. In fact, if these numbers are accurate, Hoarding Disorder is one of the most common mental health problems worldwide. You're in good company!

Special Issues in Hoarding

Insight

Many people with hoarding are intensely bothered by the problem. They recognize that their clutter is excessive, they feel ashamed of it, and they wish they could do something about. However, as we mentioned, some people show a surprising lack of awareness of just how bad the problem is. We have heard lots of people, even those with very severe problems, say things like, "What's the big deal? It's not that messy." Or, "I don't have anything in my house that I don't absolutely need." Alternatively, the person might sometimes acknowledge that there is a problem, but at other times he or she asserts that nothing is wrong. In many cases, it is the person's family members who contact us, often at their wits' end, because their loved one either cannot or will not acknowledge the problem. Odds are high that if you have read this far in this book, you have some good insight that the hoarding is really a problem. But you, like many others, may feel more than a little ambivalent about fixing it. We will talk more about this issue in Chapters 4 and 6.

Disorganization

In addition to excessive acquiring and difficulty throwing items away, people with hoarding usually have trouble keeping their possessions organized. For most people, possessions are organized by categories: linens belong in the linen closet, canned food belongs in the cupboards, tax returns belong in a file drawer, and so forth. But many people with hoarding problems don't use categories to organize their possessions. For example, you might put the tax returns on top of the pile, a little off to the left where you can see them. This provides a memory cue and gives you some confidence that you can find it when needed. Unfortunately, though, the result is a mixture of important and unimportant things randomly distributed throughout the pile. Over time, new possessions cover the previous layer of the pile, and you are left with only a rough mental map of where things are located in the pile. If anyone else touches or moves anything in the pile, your mental map is ruined. This method of organizing relies on visual and spatial memory and makes it difficult to keep track of, much less use, your possessions for their intended purpose.

Fact File for Family and Friends

A word to family members and other loved ones: Many of the people reading this book have a loved one with a hoarding problem. Often, the person agrees with you that the problem exists and that something needs to be done about it. However, for many of you, your loved one (who might be smart, logical, and rational in every other way) denies or minimizes this problem. This can be maddening for families. We have lost count of how many family members have asked, in exasperation, "Doesn't she see it?" or "Why doesn't he just clean up this mess?" Later in this book, we will suggest some specific ways to talk to your loved one about the hoarding problem. For now, recognize that his or her denial or minimization is part of the problem and is a common feature of hoarding.

Unsanitary Conditions

For some people, hoarding involves more than just clutter: there's a distinctly unsanitary element to their home. Rotten food is strewn around; mold and mildew are growing on the walls; animal, or even human, urine or feces go uncleaned. Sometimes the person is disheveled and has a strong body odor (although in other cases the person has a very tidy and clean personal appearance). A condition called Diogenes syndrome, often seen in people who have had strokes or other injuries to the brain, has a very similar presentation. It is not clear, however, whether people with hoarding problems characterized by squalor have the same kind of brain abnormalities. This type of problem often requires special attention from human service professionals.

Animal Hoarding

When animals are present in a hoarding situation, living conditions can deteriorate rapidly. Sometimes animals are collected and hoarded in addition to, or instead of, objects. We have known people who had 30, 80, even 100 cats or dogs living with them. In these cases the health and safety of the animals, as well as that of their owners and others living nearby, can be seriously threatened. In response to this growing problem, the Hoarding of Animals Research Consortium (HARC) was formed in the late 1990s to increase awareness of this problem and to stimulate research on the psychological and sociological basis for animal hoarding. HARC defines animal hoarding not by the number of animals but by the failure to recognize the animals' needs and inadequate care given to animals (see breakout box). What follows is an example of someone with an animal hoarding problem.

For more information about HARC, visit their Web site at www.tufts.edu/vet/cfa/hoarding.

＊ *Pam is a 53-year-old single woman who completed college but is unemployed. She lives with her 85-year-old mother and her 35 cats. She has had as many as 75 cats at one time. Her house is heavily cluttered and has a strong ammonia smell, and remnants of cat feces can be seen smeared on some of the walls. Pam does not notice the smell. While she notices the feces smeared on the wall, she says she just doesn't have enough time to keep up with the cleaning. Over the years she has gotten into trouble with the Humane Society and the Society for the Prevention of Cruelty to Animals over the condition of her animals. She insists it is not the number of cats that is the problem, but the fact that sometimes things just get "a little messy." Still, she insists that her cats are loved and well cared for, saying, "They live better than I do." Pam identifies herself as an animal lover, and her attachment to her cats is intensely emotional. She believes they provide her with love that she has not found elsewhere in life. She began collecting cats when someone at an animal shelter told her that the shelter euthanized 50 cats every day. At that point she started taking cats from the shelter until she got more than she could handle. Still, Pam refused to give up any of the animals. In her view, they were better off with her than going to an animal shelter where they might be euthanized.*

According to HARC, animal hoarding has four characteristics:

- *Having more* than the typical number of companion animals
- *Failure* to provide minimal standards of nutrition, sanitation, shelter, and veterinary care for the animals
- *Persistence* in accumulating more animals
- *Denial* or minimization of problems for animals, people, and living conditions.

Hoarding Among Older People

In our clinical and research programs, we tend to see a greater-than-expected number of older people. With an average age of about 50 for most people who hoard, it is not surprising that a number of our clients and research participants are over 65. Older people with hoarding problems face several special challenges. Their energy level and stamina may be limited and their physical strength may not be sufficient to tackle big sorting and cleaning tasks. They may be at greater risk of clutter-related health problems such as falling or respiratory illness. In some cases, they suffer from dementia, strokes, or other problems of the brain that make it difficult to concentrate, focus, and remember things.

✳ Is Hoarding Related to Other Psychiatric Disorders?

Hoarding is recognized as a diagnosable (and treatable) behavioral syndrome and is considered a psychiatric disorder. However, there is some disagreement about where it "fits" among other disorders. Historically, most clinicians and researchers grouped hoarding with obsessive-compulsive disorder (OCD). In the most recent edition of the *Diagnostic and Statistical Manual of Mental Disorders*, Hoarding Disorder is grouped in a section called "OCD

and Related Disorders"—meaning the authors of the DSM still consider hoarding to be *related* to OCD, even if they no longer consider it to be the same as OCD. OCD is an anxiety disorder characterized by unwanted and scary thoughts and repetitive, uncontrollable behaviors called compulsions or rituals. Certainly, some aspects of hoarding seem consistent with OCD. People with hoarding sometimes feel afraid to throw things away, worry excessively, and repeatedly check to make sure they're not throwing away anything important. However, other aspects of hoarding seem very inconsistent with OCD. For example, OCD is not usually associated with pleasurable experiences, but people who hoard often feel pleasure when they acquire and when they discover special items amidst the clutter. In our research, most people with Hoarding Disorder didn't have "classic" OCD symptoms such as washing, checking, or repeating. Our research using brain scans and other tests (which we'll discuss later on) also suggests that at a biological level, OCD and Hoarding Disorder have different patterns of brain activity. For these reasons, we suspect that Hoarding Disorder and OCD are quite distinct.

Depression is another condition that seems to occur commonly along with hoarding. Most cases of hoarding do not appear to result from depression, but many people with hoarding get depressed, perhaps because of their hoarding problem. People who feel severely and chronically depressed typically have low energy, lack of motivation, and difficulty concentrating. These symptoms can get in the way of doing the work necessary to get over the hoarding problem.

Other people with hoarding show features of attention-deficit/hyperactivity disorder (ADHD). Specifically, they have difficulty staying focused on tasks and are easily distracted. This makes it difficult to engage in prolonged sorting and decluttering.

We have also seen a high rate of anxiety disorders, most notably generalized anxiety disorder and social anxiety disorder, among people with Hoarding Disorder. Many people who hoard feel chronically worried and on edge, and they may have difficulty concentrating or feel tired and cranky

Diagnostic Criteria for ADHD

Either six or more of the following symptoms of inattention or six or more of the following symptoms of hyperactivity/impulsivity must be present:

Symptoms of Inattention

Often fails to give close attention to details or makes careless mistakes in schoolwork, work, or other activities

Often has difficulty sustaining attention in tasks or play activities

Often does not seem to listen when spoken to directly

Often does not follow through on instructions and fails to finish schoolwork, chores, or duties in the workplace (not because of oppositional behavior or failure to understand instructions)

Often has difficulty organizing tasks and activities

Often avoids, dislikes, or is reluctant to engage in tasks that require sustained mental effort

Often loses things necessary for tasks or activities

Is often easily distracted by extraneous stimuli

Is often forgetful in daily activities

Symptoms of Hyperactivity/Impulsivity

Often fidgets with hands or feet or squirms in seat

Often leaves seat in classroom or in other situations in which remaining seated is expected

Often runs about or climbs excessively in situations in which it is inappropriate (in adolescents or adults, may be limited to subjective feelings of restlessness)

Often has difficulty playing or engaging in leisure activities quietly

Is often "on the go" or often acts as if "driven by a motor"

Often talks excessively

Often blurts out answers before questions have been completed

Often has difficulty awaiting turn

Often interrupts or intrudes on others

much of the time. Some are shy and nervous around other people and tend to have fewer social interactions. As a result, they may be less motivated to clean their homes because they are uncomfortable inviting others in. They also may feel more ashamed of the problem and therefore less likely to reach out for help.

Additional Resources

Treatments *ThatWork*™

Mastering Your Adult ADHD

Mastery of Your Anxiety and Worry, Second Edition

Treating Your OCD with Exposure and Response (Ritual) Prevention, Second Edition

Managing Social Anxiety

Oxford University Press

3

Do I Have a Problem
With Hoarding?

Since you purchased this book, you probably already have a pretty good idea about whether or not you have a hoarding problem. This chapter will help you determine how serious your problem is. By answering the questions on the following pages, you will learn the overall severity of your hoarding problem (Hoarding Rating Scale), whether it compromises your safety (Is My Home Safe?), the extent to which hoarding interferes with your daily activities (Are Your Daily Activities Impaired by Hoarding?), and whether there are problems with sanitation in your home (Home Environment Index). Complete each of these questionnaires to get a baseline of your hoarding. We will ask you to complete them again at the end (Chapter 13) so you can see the progress you have made with this program.

●✇ Hoarding Rating Scale

Use the following test to find out if you have a problem with hoarding. For each question below, circle the number that corresponds most closely to your experience **DURING THE PAST WEEK.**

1. Because of the clutter or number of possessions, how difficult is it for you to use the rooms in your home?

0	1	2	3	4	5	6	7	8
Not at all difficult		Mildly difficult		Moderately difficult		Severely difficult		Extremely difficult

2. To what extent do you have difficulty discarding (or recycling, selling, giving away) ordinary things that other people would get rid of?

0	1	2	3	4	5	6	7	8
No difficulty		Mild difficulty		Moderate difficulty		Severe difficulty		Extreme difficulty

3. To what extent do you currently have a problem with collecting free things or buying more things than you need or can use or can afford?

0	1	2	3	4	5	6	7	8
No problem		Mild problem		Moderate problem		Severe problem		Extreme problem

4. To what extent do you experience emotional distress because of clutter, difficulty discarding, or problems with buying or acquiring things?

0	1	2	3	4	5	6	7	8
None		Mild		Moderate		Severe		Extreme

5. To what extent do you experience impairment in your life (daily routine, job/school, social activities, family activities, financial difficulties) because of clutter, difficulty discarding, or problems with buying or acquiring things?

0	1	2	3	4	5	6	7	8
None		Mild		Moderate		Severe		Extreme

Generally speaking, we consider an issue to be significant when your response is 4 (moderate) or greater. If your score on items 1 (clutter), 2 (difficulty discarding), or 3 (acquiring) was 4 or higher, that suggests that at least some symptoms of hoarding are significant for you.

In addition, if your score on items 4 (distress) or 5 (impairment) was 4 or higher, that means that the symptoms of hoarding are having a real impact on your quality of life.

Safety is a concern when hoarding is severe. Answer these questions to determine whether there are safety issues you need to address.

Type of problem	None	Somewhat/A little	moderate	Substantial	Severe
1. Is there any structural damage to the floors, walls, roof, or other parts of your home?	1	2	3	4	5
2. Does any part of your house pose a fire hazard (e.g., stove covered with paper, flammable objects near the furnace, etc.)?	1	2	3	4	5
3. Are parts of your house unsanitary (bathrooms unclean, strong odor)?	1	2	3	4	5
4. Would medical emergency personnel have difficulty moving equipment through your home?	1	2	3	4	5
5. Are any exits from your home blocked?	1	2	3	4	5
6. Is it unsafe to move up or down the stairs or along other walkways?	1	2	3	4	5
7. Is there clutter outside your house (porch, yard, alleyway, common areas if apartment or condo)?	1	2	3	4	5

Add your scores for items 1–7. _____

This is your *Safety* score.

Your scores can be classified as:

7-13	Minimal
14-20	Mild
21-27	Moderate
28-30	Severe
31-35	Very severe

If you scored 21 or higher (moderate or worse), you may be living in an unsafe home. If you scored 3 or higher on any one question, this should be a high priority item to be addressed right away.

➤ Are Your Daily Activities Impaired by Hoarding?

Sometimes clutter in the home can prevent you from doing ordinary activities. For each of the following activities, please circle the number that best represents how much difficulty you experience in doing this activity because of the clutter or hoarding problem. If you have difficulty with the activity for other reasons (for example, physical problems make it hard for you to pick things up or walk easily), do not include this problem in your rating. Instead, rate only how much difficulty you have due to hoarding. If the activity is not relevant to your situation (for example, you don't have laundry facilities or animals), check the Not Applicable (NA) box.

Activities affected by clutter or hoarding problem	Can do it easily	Can do it with a little difficulty	Can do it with moderate difficulty	Can do it with great difficulty	Unable to do	NA
1. Prepare food	1	2	3	4	5	NA
2. Use refrigerator	1	2	3	4	5	NA
3. Use stove	1	2	3	4	5	NA
4. Use kitchen sink	1	2	3	4	5	NA
5. Eat at table	1	2	3	4	5	NA
6. Move around inside the house	1	2	3	4	5	NA
7. Exit home quickly	1	2	3	4	5	NA
8. Use toilet	1	2	3	4	5	NA

Activities affected by clutter or hoarding problem	Can do it easily	Can do it with a little difficulty	Can do it with moderate difficulty	Can do it with great difficulty	Unable to do	NA
9. Use bath/shower	1	2	3	4	5	NA
10. Use bathroom sink	1	2	3	4	5	NA
11. Answer door quickly	1	2	3	4	5	NA
12. Sit in sofa/chair	1	2	3	4	5	NA
13. Sleep in bed	1	2	3	4	5	NA
14. Do laundry	1	2	3	4	5	NA
15. Find important things (such as bills, tax forms, etc.)	1	2	3	4	5	NA

These questions assess the extent to which clutter causes problems in daily functioning at home.

Step 1: Add your scores for items 1–15, excluding the items with NA (not applicable) ratings. _____

Step 2: Count how many questions (up to 15) you answered with a numeric score (not an NA rating). _____

Step 3: Divide the first number by the second number.

_____

For example, if your total score for items 1–15 was 45, and you gave numeric ratings for 14 items (meaning you made 1 NA rating), your score is 45 ÷ 14 = 3.21. This is your *Activities of Daily Living* score.

Your scores can be classified as:

1.0–1.4   Minimal
1.5–2.0   Mild
2.1–3.0   Moderate
3.1–4.0   Severe
4.1–5.0   Very severe

If you scored 2.1 or higher (moderate or worse), the clutter has caused substantial difficulties in your ability to function in your home.

Does Hoarding Affect the Sanitary Condition of Your Home?

Clutter and hoarding problems can sometimes lead to sanitation problems. Please circle the answer that best fits the current situation in the home.

To what extent are the following situations present in the home?

1. Fire hazard

    0 = No fire hazard
    1 = Some risk of fire (for example, lots of flammable material)
    2 = Moderate risk of fire (for example, flammable materials near heat source)
    3 = High risk of fire (for example, flammable materials near heat source, electrical hazards, etc.)

2. Moldy or rotten food

    0 = None
    1 = A few pieces of moldy or rotten food in kitchen
    2 = Some moldy or rotten food throughout kitchen
    3 = Large quantity of moldy or rotten food in kitchen and elsewhere

3. Dirty or clogged sink

    0 = Sink empty and clean
    1 = A few dirty dishes with water in sink
    2 = Sink full of water, possibly clogged
    3 = Sink clogged with evidence that it has overflowed onto counters, etc.

4. Standing water (in sink, tub, other container, basement, etc.)

    0 = No standing water
    1 = Some water in sink/tub
    2 = Water in several places, especially if dirty
    3 = Water in numerous places, especially if dirty

5. Human/animal waste/vomit

    0 = No human waste, animal waste, or vomit visible
    1 = Small amount of human or animal waste (e.g., unflushed toilet, on bathroom or other floor)
    2 = Moderate animal or human waste or vomit visible in more than one room
    3 = Animal or human waste or vomit on floors or other surfaces

6. Mildew or mold

    0 = No mildew or mold detectable

1 = Small amount of mildew or mold in limited amounts and expected places (for example, on edge of shower curtain or refrigerator seal)

2 = Considerable, noticeable mildew or mold

3 = Widespread mildew or mold on most surfaces

7. Dirty food containers

0 = All dishes washed and put away

1 = A few unwashed dishes

2 = Many unwashed dishes

3 = Almost all dishes are unwashed

8. Dirty surfaces (floors, walls, furniture, etc.)

0 = Surfaces completely clean

1 = A few spills, some dirt or grime

2 = More than a few spills, may be a thin covering of dirt or grime in living areas

3 = No surface is clean; dirt or grime covers everything

9. Piles of dirty or contaminated objects (bathroom tissue, hair, toilet paper, sanitary products, etc.)

0 = No dirty or contaminated objects on floors, surfaces, etc.

1 = Some dirty or contaminated objects present around trash cans or toilets

2 = Many dirty or contaminated objects fill bathroom or area around trash cans

3 = Dirty or contaminated objects cover the floors and surfaces in most rooms

10. Insects

0 = No insects are visible

1 = A few insects visible; cobwebs and/or insect droppings present

2 = Many insects and droppings are visible; cobwebs in corners

3 = Swarms of insects; high volume of droppings; many cobwebs on household items

11. Dirty clothes

0 = Dirty clothes placed in hamper; none are lying around

1 = Hamper is full; a few dirty clothes lying around

2 = Hamper is overflowing; many dirty clothes lying around

3 = Clothes cover the floor and many other surfaces (bed, chairs, etc.)

12. Dirty bed sheets/linens

0 = Bed coverings very clean

1 = Bed coverings relatively clean

2 = Bed coverings dirty and in need of washing

3 = Bed coverings very dirty and soiled

13. Odor of house

   0 = No odor
   1 = Slight odor
   2 = Moderate odor; may be strong in some parts of house
   3 = Strong odor throughout house

   During the last month, how often did you (or someone in your home) do each of the following activities?

14. Do the dishes

   0 = Daily or every 2 days; 15 to 30 times per month
   1 = 1 or 2 times a week; 4 to 10 times per month
   3 = Every other week; 2 or 3 times per month
   3 = Rarely; 0 times per month

15. Clean the bathroom

   0 = Daily or every 2 days; more than 10 times per month
   1 = 1 or 2 times a week; 4 to 10 times per month
   2 = Every other week; 2 or 3 times per month
   3 = Never; 0 times per month

To score the HEI, sum the responses for all 15 items. The average score for a large Internet sample of people with hoarding was 12.7 (standard deviation = 6.9; range = 0–43). A score of 2 or above on any question warrants attention.

Taking Pictures

Lastly, take some photographs of your home. We know that this is not fun for some people. But it's important to have a record of how things look BEFORE you start this program, so don't skip this part! Grab a camera or your cell phone, and go from room to room taking pictures of the clutter. Store these photos somewhere safe, like on your computer hard drive or on a CD or jump drive (saving them electronically helps prevent adding to the physical clutter in the home). Later on in the program, we're going to ask you to look at the pictures again so you can measure your progress.

4

Meet the Bad Guys

Have you bought books on organizing and not used them? Have you started on a program or plan to get control of your clutter and not followed through? In our experience there are ways of thinking—we call them "the bad guys"—that prevent people who hoard from benefiting from organizing books and programs. In this chapter, we're going to introduce you to five bad guys. If you're like most people who hoard, one or more of these bad guys has already taken up residence in your life. Perhaps you've been aware of it, perhaps not. But as you go through this program, it's likely that you will become increasingly aware of their presence. These bad guys represent the psychological factors that, in our experience, have been the primary obstacles to recovery for people who hoard.

Why are we introducing you to these bad guys? Because we believe that the more you understand this problem, the better equipped you will be to beat it. You may not be able to stop the bad guys from showing up, but at least you can see them coming. We will describe each of the bad guys here and provide you with some self-assessment tools to determine the extent to which they are factors in your life; in the next chapter, we'll discuss specific strategies for beating them.

> *You may not be able to stop the bad guys from showing up, but at least you can see them coming.*

Bad Guy #1: "It's just not my priority"

The number-one reason people don't overcome their hoarding problem is that they don't spend the time needed to work on the problem. For some, making this work a priority is hampered by reduced awareness of the problem. In such cases, the person is unaware, or only dimly aware, that he or she has a hoarding problem at all. He or she might say things like, "It's not that bad; I don't see what the big fuss is about" or "My house might be a little messy, but whose isn't?" We asked Bill (from Chapter 2) to draw a diagram of his house. When we actually went to visit him there, we were surprised to see that where he had drawn a wall, there was actually a wall of clutter that cut off half of the room. Bill had drawn his living room as if the cluttered half wasn't even there. Most cases aren't quite that dramatic, but we can still see elements of low awareness, such as a woman who has gotten into the habit of not looking up as she walks through her living room so she doesn't even see the condition of the room.

In other cases, however, lack of awareness is not the problem. Quite the contrary, many people who hoard are very aware and unhappy about their home. But as soon as they begin to seriously think about what it will mean to get rid of specific things they have been saving, suddenly the reasons for saving seem more important than curtailing their hoarding. Having to give up things that are useful or sentimental or otherwise have value doesn't seem to make sense and leads people to ask themselves whether their clutter and hoarding is really such a big deal. The result is that work on the hoarding problem is relegated to the bottom of the list of things to do, which means it doesn't get done.

Regardless of whether this bad guy takes the form of reduced awareness or not making control of hoarding a priority, it comes down to a simple formula: *people start to work on their hoarding problem when the reasons for change outweigh the reasons for not changing, and not a minute sooner.* In Figure 4.1, you see a scale that we'll call the "balance of change." On one side are potential reasons for working on the hoarding problem. Not all of these will necessarily apply to you; we have borrowed these from many people we have assessed in our research programs. On the other side are potential reasons for *not* working on the hoarding problem. It's important to recognize both of these. When the person's reasons for not changing are more numerous or seem more important than the reasons for changing, you can bet that the person is not ready to work on the problem, and that attempts to do so will likely end in frustration. However, when the person's reasons for changing outweigh the reasons for not changing, he or she is ready to get to work.

Reasons to change

- Clutter is hurting my social life.
- My hoarding problem makes me feel bad about myself.
- My family argues a lot about my hoarding problem.
- I want to get my life under control.
- I want to feel comfortable in my own home.
- All of this clutter is not safe for me.
- People would get off my back if I could improve this situation.
- I want to set a better example for my kids and give them a better living environment.
- I need to work on the problem in order to avoid legal problems.
- I'd have a lot more money if I could cut back on acquiring.

Reasons not to change

- My clutter's not hurting anyone.
- Working on the problem would be like "giving in" to people who have been nagging me.
- Acquiring is one of the few things that bring me pleasure.
- I'm perfectly happy with things as they are.
- Acknowledging the problem would make me feel bad.
- Nothing's worked before, so why bother trying?
- Eventually I'll just get a bigger home that all my stuff can fit into.
- I couldn't stand doing a difficult program.
- I just don't have the time.

Figure 4.1 The Balance of Change Scale.

Now we'd like you to take a moment to determine your own readiness for change. Remember, this will be most useful if you actually get a pencil or pen right now and write in the book.

●◁ Are You Ready to Change?

Each statement describes how a person might feel when thinking about hoarding. Please indicate the extent to which you tend to agree or disagree with each statement. In each case, make your choice in terms of how you feel RIGHT NOW, not how you have felt in the past or would like to feel. Be honest now.

There are FIVE possible responses to each of the items in the questionnaire:

1	2	3	4	5
Strongly Disagree (SD)	Disagree (D)	Undecided (U)	Agree (A)	Strongly Agree (SA)

	SD	D	U	A	SA
1. As far as I'm concerned, I don't have a hoarding problem that needs changing.	1	2	3	4	5
2. I'm not the one with the problem. It doesn't make sense for me to be doing this program.	1	2	3	4	5
3. I have a problem with hoarding and I really think I should work on it.	1	2	3	4	5
4. I'm hoping this program will help me to better understand myself and my hoarding.	1	2	3	4	5
5. I am doing something about hoarding.	1	2	3	4	5
6. Anyone can talk about changing; I'm actually doing something about it.	1	2	3	4	5
7. It worries me that I might slip back on the gains I have already made in hoarding, so I am hoping this program will help.	1	2	3	4	5
8. I thought once I had resolved hoarding I would be free of it, but sometimes I still find myself struggling with it.	1	2	3	4	5

Add your responses to items 1 and 2: _____ This is your "Not ready for it" score.

Add your responses to items 3 and 4: _____ This is your "Thinking about it" score.

Add your responses to items 5 and 6: _____ This is your "Working on it" score.

Add your responses to items 7 and 8: _____ This is your "Keeping the ball rolling" score.

Which of the four scores was highest? If your highest score was "Not ready for it," this suggests that you do not believe that you have a problem, or that you are not particularly invested in changing. If your highest score was

"Thinking about it," you are aware that a problem exists, and that it bothers you. However, you might not yet have made a strong commitment to do something about it. If your highest score was "Working on it," you have actively started to work on hoarding, although you may not yet have been entirely successful in managing it. If your highest score was "Keeping the ball rolling," you have already made significant progress on hoarding but might still need help making sure you stay on the right path.

(Adapted from McConnaughy, E. A., Prochaska, J. O., & Velicer, W. F. (1983). Stages of change in psychotherapy: Measurement and sample profiles. *Psychotherapy: Theory, Research, and Practice, 20,* 368–375.)

Bad Guy #2: Letting Unhelpful Beliefs Get in Your Way

People with hoarding often have beliefs, sometimes very strong ones, about their possessions. Many of these beliefs are not unusual in and of themselves; in fact, most people, even those without hoarding problems, think this way from time to time. However, for people with hoarding, the beliefs have become so strong, so intense, or so inflexible that they have become unhelpful. These beliefs are likely to get in the way of your progress; therefore, we have added them to our list of bad guys. Unhelpful beliefs can take several forms, including the following.

Beliefs About Usefulness

When Bill looked around his home, he saw all kinds of opportunities: a broken TV that he might be able to fix and put in his bedroom, a case of light bulbs that he hoped to sell at a flea market, and so on. On one hand, we might admire Bill for his ability to think of ways to use things that others might call junk, as well as his entrepreneurial spirit. Remember, however, that in cases of hoarding, the beliefs have stopped being helpful and have become *un*helpful. When we asked Bill some more detailed questions, we found out that that broken TV set had been sitting in his living room for 4 years. It was obvious to everyone (except, perhaps, Bill) that he was not going to fix it. And those light bulbs that he planned to sell at a flea market? When we opened the box, we found that many of them were broken after sitting in a pile of clutter for over a year. Furthermore, not only had Bill never sold anything at a flea market, he didn't even know where one was.

Sometimes, unhelpful beliefs about the usefulness of objects lead a person to confuse "needing" with "wanting." To need something means that you cannot do without it: for example, human beings need food, water, oxygen, shelter, and so on. Without these things, great harm would come to us. We do not, however, *need* most of the things in our homes; rather, we *want* them, meaning we feel better having them. Have you ever found yourself saying, "I need this" or "I might need this someday"? If so, did you really mean *need,* or *want*?

Perfectionism and Fear of Making Mistakes

Helen (from Chapter 2) also had unhelpful beliefs about her possessions, although her beliefs were different from Bill's. When she looked around her home, she didn't see opportunities for putting things to use. Instead, she saw the potential to make mistakes, with disastrous consequences. When she picked up a piece of mail, she didn't feel a sense of excitement about the contents. She felt anxious, worried, and sick. She would ask herself, "What if I make a mistake? What if I make the wrong decision?" Even though her home was messy, in terms of her beliefs, Helen was what many people would call a perfectionist. In fact, her perfectionism—her fear of making mistakes—was so strong that it led her to avoid making decisions altogether.

Perfectionism is a serious motivation-killer. During the Buried in Treasures Workshops we conducted, we noticed that a lot of people reported feeling like a failure, even when they were making good progress. Remember that any behavioral change—whether it's losing weight, quitting smoking, learning to drive, or getting hoarding under control—is usually a slow process, with significant ups and downs along the way. Sometimes you seem to be chugging along well; other times the progress seems slower. When you notice partial progress, try to keep it in perspective. You can kick yourself for not going faster, doing better, getting it just right, and so on—or you can congratulate yourself for the progress that you *are* making. Of course, we're not advocating putting on rose-colored glasses; if something is getting in your way or slowing you down, it's important to recognize it and deal with it as best you can. But watch out for unhelpful beliefs about being a failure. Sometimes, progress will be slow or hard to see. Don't despair.

Beliefs About Responsibility

Similar to perfectionism, many people with hoarding problems feel an exaggerated sense of responsibility to make sure that possessions get used, disposed of, or donated in exactly the right way. Again, there's nothing inherently wrong with this belief; most of us would want to see our possessions go to a "good home," or would like to see things recycled properly, and so on. But, like the other beliefs, when the sense of responsibility becomes rigid, inflexible, or excessively cumbersome, it becomes one of the bad guys. When you tell yourself, "I'd be willing to part with this object as long as I know it's going to a good home," that suggests that even though you might be willing on some level to let it go, at an emotional level you're not ready to detach yourself from it. You still feel responsible for it, even after you let go of it.

We asked Helen to gather some old toys from her basement and bring them to a local charity store where they would be resold and the proceeds donated to a variety of charitable causes. She loaded the toys into her car and drove to the store. However, when she got there, she had second thoughts: "Is this the best charity? How do I know the money will go to causes I support? Wouldn't it be better for me to donate these toys directly to some needy children?" In response to these thoughts, Helen put the toys back in her car and went home. She was starting to feel tired and confused, and thought, "I'll put these toys back in the basement until I can figure out what to do with them." Instead of helping her take positive action, her perfectionistic beliefs got in her way.

Attachments to Possessions

In its proper context, attachment is what makes us feel good around people we love and who love us. It gives us a sense of friendship, affiliation, or love. However, when the attachment to objects becomes excessive, we have a difficult time letting go of things that are no longer useful to us. Many people who hoard feel a strong sense of attachment to the objects in their homes. This sense of attachment is not all that unusual; however, any beliefs, when taken to an extreme or applied inflexibly, can become a problem. We went with Bill on one of his "treasure hunts," looking for discarded furniture on the side of the road. Pulling over at a coffee table that someone had thrown away, Bill started talking about not only how he could refinish it and perhaps sell it, but also how he felt like the table needed "rescuing." It was as if this inanimate object was a living thing, with feelings, and that he some-how had to make this poor thing feel better by taking it. Helen had some attachment beliefs of her own. Her parents had passed away about 5 years prior, and she inherited many of the things from their home. Some of these things would likely have sentimental value for anyone—photo albums, her mother's favorite dress, and so forth. But among these truly sentimental objects were many items most people would not find sentimental or useful. For example, she had inherited her parents' toaster, which she had placed next to her own (better) toaster on the kitchen counter. When we asked her about it, she said, "I know I don't need another toaster, but I just feel I should hang on to it. It reminds me of my parents, and it would just feel like if I threw it away, I'd be throwing *them* away, too."

Beliefs About Objects as a Source of Identity

For many people with hoarding problems, possessions serve as reminders of who they are—or, in many cases, who they want to be. Bill is a great example of this kind of belief. A creative man, Bill imagined himself to be an entrepreneur, picking up free or inexpensive things and then selling them for a profit. But remember that Bill's activities were limited to acquiring things; in fact, he was so busy acquiring that he never made it to the potentially profitable part of his venture, selling. Like so many people with hoarding problems, Bill was defining himself not by what he *did,* but rather by what he *had* and what he *hoped to do.* Take a moment and think about whether you derive a sense of identity from your possessions. Do the things in your home make you feel like a businessperson? A crafter? An artist? A handyperson? A parent? A good friend? Now ask yourself: is the amount I *have* proportional to the amount I *do*?

Underestimating Memory

It's quite common for people to leave things in sight so they don't forget about them. For example, if we have a bill that needs to be paid, we might leave it on the kitchen counter as a reminder. Some people with hoard-ing, however, seriously underestimate their own memory capacity. They have become so used to relying on visual reminders that they have lost confidence in their own ability to remember things. As a result, they leave "reminders" everywhere. Eventually, the "reminders" don't really remind them of anything because they all blur together.

Beliefs About Control

Sometimes, decisions about discarding, saving, and acquiring get tangled up with our beliefs about independence and autonomy. If you're like a lot of the people we've met who hoard, you might have had the experience of family members, friends, even healthcare or social service workers telling you what to do with your possessions. It's quite understandable that these experiences can make you feel angry or resentful—after all, it's *your* stuff. The tricky part is knowing how to handle those kinds of thoughts and feelings. All too often, people respond by doing things that are self-damaging. They might respond by acting stubbornly, digging in their heels and resisting making any changes. Sometimes they might even respond by doing the exact *opposite* of what they're being asked or told to do! Bill's adult daughter came to his house, yelling and nagging at him to get rid of his possessions. When she left, Bill felt angry and thought, "No one's gonna tell me what to do." He responded by going out and acquiring *more* items. On one hand, Bill was making a statement that he was not going to be controlled by someone else. On the other hand, through this behavior, Bill ultimately was only hurting himself by adding to his clutter.

What Do You Believe?

Use the following scale to indicate the extent to which you had each thought when you were deciding whether to throw something away **DURING THE PAST WEEK.** (If you did not try to discard anything in the past week, indicate how you would have felt if you had tried to discard.)

1	2	3	4	5	6	7
not at all			sometimes			very much

1. If I can think of a use for a possession, I should keep it. 1 2 3 4 5 6 7

2. I really need this. 1 2 3 4 5 6 7

3. I'd better save this because I will probably need it sometime. 1 2 3 4 5 6 7

4. I can't bear the thought of making the wrong decision. 1 2 3 4 5 6 7

5. I need to make sure that this gets handled in exactly the right way.   1 2 3 4 5 6 7

6. If I make a mistake, the results could be disastrous.   1 2 3 4 5 6 7

7. Throwing this away means wasting a valuable opportunity.   1 2 3 4 5 6 7

8. I am responsible for finding a use for this possession.   1 2 3 4 5 6 7

9. If this possession may be of use to someone else, I am responsible for saving it for him or her.   1 2 3 4 5 6 7

10. Throwing away this possession is like throwing away a part of me.   1 2 3 4 5 6 7

11. This possession provides me with emotional comfort.   1 2 3 4 5 6 7

12. I love some of my belongings the way I love some people.   1 2 3 4 5 6 7

13. My possessions help identify who I am.   1 2 3 4 5 6 7

14. Hanging on to these things is part of what makes me the person I want to be.   1 2 3 4 5 6 7

15. Having these things reminds me of activities that I hope to do.   1 2 3 4 5 6 7

16. Saving this means I don't have to rely on my memory.   1 2 3 4 5 6 7

17. My memory is so bad I must leave this in sight or I'll forget about it.   1 2 3 4 5 6 7

18. If I put this into a filing system, I'll forget about it completely.   1 2 3 4 5 6 7

19. It upsets me when someone throws something of mine away without my permission.   1 2 3 4 5 6 7

20. I like to maintain sole control over my things.   1 2 3 4 5 6 7

21. No one has the right to touch my possessions.   1 2 3 4 5 6 7

Add up your responses to items 1–3: _____ This score reflects your *beliefs about usefulness.*

Add up your responses to items 4–6: _____ This score reflects your *beliefs about perfectionism and fear of making mistakes.*

Add up your responses to items 7–9: _____ This score reflects your *beliefs about responsibility.*

Add up your responses to items 10–12: _____ This score reflects your *beliefs about attachment.*

Add up your responses to items 13–15: _____ This score reflects your *beliefs about objects as a source of identity.*

Add up your responses to items 16–18: _____ This score reflects your *beliefs about underestimating memory.*

Add up your responses to items 19–21: _____ This score reflects your *beliefs about control.*

For each of these scores, your scores can be classified as:

3–6:	Low
7–15:	Moderate
16–21:	High

(Portions of this measure were adapted from Steketee, G., Frost, R. O., & Kyrios, M. (2003). Beliefs about possessions among compulsive hoarders. *Cognitive Therapy and Research, 27,* 467–479.)

Bad Guy #3: Overthinking or Confusing Yourself

People with hoarding often run into trouble because of their intelligence and creativity. One way this occurs is when the person engages in *over-creativity*—the tendency to think of more and more uses for an object. Most of us tend to discard an item when we can no longer think of a good reason to keep it. For example, when we finish using a roll of toilet paper, we don't usually think about ways to use the cardboard tube, so we throw it away or recycle it without thinking twice about it. If, on the other hand, we put our minds to it, we could come up with lots of clever ideas. It could become a pretend telescope for children. It could be put into a hamster cage for hamsters to crawl through. It could be used as a toothbrush holder. Yarn or string could be wrapped around it for storage. Several tubes could be used as building blocks for play houses or castles. The possibilities are virtually endless. The problem for people with hoarding is that they tend to be much better at thinking of these ideas than they are at carrying them out. Those clever ideas, which seemed so compelling at that time, eventually fade, but the clutter remains.

Another form of overthinking can start to interfere even after the person has decided to get rid of something. Helen did not want all of the old newspapers and magazines that cluttered her home, but the process of getting rid of them was so elaborate that she long ago gave up trying. She had to create newspaper and magazine bundles of a certain size, tied carefully with special string, and without any wrinkles. Her reasoning had to do with the optimal size for a bundle to be handled easily, the best way to ensure the bundles did not come apart while being transported, and her beliefs about what the recycling crew would think about her if they saw disheveled piles of crumpled papers in her recycling bin. It became so difficult for her to meet these exacting standards that she simply let the papers and magazines pile up. Here you can also see beliefs about perfectionism and responsibility rearing their ugly heads.

Helen's overthinking was also apparent in her overly elaborate and cumbersome efforts to categorize her possessions. When we asked her to sort some of her mail, we could see the problem immediately. Instead of making a few piles (for example, "junk mail," "bills I need to pay," "personal correspondence," etc.), each containing lots of pieces of mail, Helen instead made lots of very small piles. She explained, "These are credit card offers with 0% financing. These are credit card offers with low rates, but not 0%. These are credit card offers with high rates. These are magazine subscription offers. These are charity solicitations," and so on. As you can see, Helen had difficulty putting things together in broad categories (many of us would classify all these as "junk mail," or at least lump them together as "financial junk mail"), and as a result she created a very burdensome task for herself. Helen's complex sorting strategy exceeded her capacity to sustain her attention and focus. She told us, "I can't seem to focus long enough to get anything done. I'll start off with the best of intentions, and really want to do something about the problem, but then I get distracted or I start thinking about something else and I forget what I was doing." Her overthinking made the sorting task so hard she couldn't continue.

Bill also had overthinking problems, but of a different sort. Unlike Helen, who had difficulty sustaining attention and was easily distracted, Bill would become so hyper-focused on an object he wanted to acquire that he could scarcely think about anything else. He told us, "When I see something I want to pick up, it's like I space out and nothing else matters. I'm in the zone." He was overthinking about all of the great things he could do with the object, while also *under*thinking about the consequences of his actions (such as whether he really needed it or had space to store it).

Use the following scale to indicate the extent to which you had each thought when you were deciding whether to throw something away **DURING THE PAST WEEK.** (If you did not try to discard anything in the past week, indicate how you would have felt if you had tried to discard.)

1	2	3	4	5	6	7
not at all			sometimes			very much

1. I can think of a lot of ways to use this.   1 2 3 4 5 6 7

2. I bet I could think of someone who could use this.   1 2 3 4 5 6 7

3. I could take this apart and use it for new projects.   1 2 3 4 5 6 7

4. There's a right and wrong way to dispose of things.   1 2 3 4 5 6 7

5. Disposing of this will take a lot of steps.   1 2 3 4 5 6 7

6. I have to make sure this gets disposed of in exactly the right way.   1 2 3 4 5 6 7

7. I just can't decide what category this should go in.   1 2 3 4 5 6 7

8. If two items are a little bit different, they should go in different categories.   1 2 3 4 5 6 7

9. Statements from two different credit cards should be put in different categories so I don't get them mixed up.   1 2 3 4 5 6 7

Add your responses to items 1–3: _____ This score reflects your tendency to be *overly creative.*

Add your responses to items 4–6: _____ This score reflects your tendency to use a *cumbersome process* for letting go of things.

Add your responses to items 7–9: _____ This score reflects your tendency to *overcategorize.*

For each of these scores, your scores can be classified as:

    3–6:   Low
    7–15:   Moderate
   16–21: High

Bad Guy #4: Avoidance and Excuse-Making

Avoidance might be the most deadly of the bad guys. Quite often, the prospect of discarding brings up powerful feelings such as sadness and anxiety. There's nothing wrong with having these feelings; in fact, they're part of what makes us human. But how we react to those feelings can be a major problem. Let's face it, sadness and anxiety are unpleasant, but for many people these feelings become so aversive, so intolerable, that they go to great lengths to avoid them. Helen's perfectionistic beliefs, which we described earlier in this chapter, led her to feel terrified at the prospect of making a mistake. She imagined throwing away a bill she needed to pay and then her mind generated all sorts of awful consequences of her mistake. She imagined the bill would become overdue, additional late charges would be applied, the bill would be referred to a collection agency, her credit report would be ruined, the creditor would put a lien on her house, and eventually she would go bankrupt. A healthy response to these worries might be to work out a method to pay her bills on time. An unhealthy response, the one Helen chose, was to stop looking through her mail because it made her feel anxious. Instead of channeling her anxiety into positive, active behavior that would make her situation better, she instead tried to avoid her anxiety (by ignoring her mail); this made her feel better but didn't actually improve her situation at all. In fact, avoidance ended up making her situation much worse.

Sometimes we avoid things not because they make us feel sad or anxious, but rather because they make us feel overwhelmed and confused. Recall how Helen's overthinking led her to become confused about what to do and where to begin. Whenever she even looked at the clutter in her home, she began to feel a strong sense of fatigue, like she needed to lie down. She would tell herself, "I just can't do this right now. I'm just too tired and stressed out. Besides, I'm too busy to really work on the problem right now; there just isn't time. I'll deal with it later, when I'm feeling more up to it." Helen was using her feelings of fatigue, stress, and lack of time as excuses to procrastinate. Not surprisingly, her excuse-making and procrastination were not helping her solve the problem—quite the contrary, they were some of the main things that allowed the clutter to keep piling up. There was no way around it: for Helen's problem to get better, she was going to have to face some uncomfortable feelings.

⚷ Do You Avoid and Make Excuses?

Use the following scale to indicate the extent to which you had each thought when you were deciding whether to throw something away **DURING THE PAST WEEK.** (If you did not try to discard anything in the past week, indicate how you would have felt if you had tried to discard.)

1	2	3	4	5	6	7
not at all			sometimes			very much

1. I'm just too tired to do this right now.　　1　2　3　4　5　6　7

2. I'm too stressed out to even think about this.　　1　2　3　4　5　6　7

3. I don't have enough energy to work on this problem.　　1　2　3　4　5　6　7

4. I'll get to it later.　　1　2　3　4　5　6　7

5. I just have too many demands on my time to do this.　　1　2　3　4　5　6　7

6. My health is a problem and might prevent me from working on this.　　1　2　3　4　5　6　7

7. This just makes me feel too anxious; I can't do it.　　1　2　3　4　5　6　7

8. I can't stand the possibility of feeling bad, so I'll put it off.　　1　2　3　4　5　6　7

9. I'll get to this as soon as I fix some other problems in my life.　　1　2　3　4　5　6　7

If you circled 4 or higher for *any* item on this measure, it sounds like avoidance and excuse-making might be a problem for you. If you circled 4 or higher on *more than one* item, then avoidance and excuse-making might be a very significant problem that you will have to face head on as you go through this program.

Bad Guy #5: Going for the Short-Term Payoff

Without a sense of pleasure, life becomes very boring and depressing. People with hoarding often find that their ability to derive pleasure is limited to acquiring possessions—that is, acquiring has become one of the only ways to feel happy. Bill described this kind of pleasure when he went out and found a "treasure" or "bargain." Of course, the pleasure is usually short-lived and pales in comparison to the long-term unhappiness that comes from excessive clutter and restriction of other fun social activities. People with hoarding problems often experience positive emotions when acquiring, such as the thrill of finding a bargain or the emotional satisfaction of rescuing a lost treasure. You might well ask, "So what? That's not unusual; everybody likes finding a bargain or acquiring something they like." This is true, and it leads to another part of the picture: for most of us, successfully navigating life means striking the right balance between what *feels* good and what *is* good. Should we have a salad or a piece of chocolate cake? Should we exercise, or watch TV? There isn't necessarily a right or wrong answer; it depends on the person and situation. But living a balanced and successful life does involve, at least some of the time, inhibiting things that are immediately reinforcing and instead choosing things that will pay off in the long run. Another way of saying this is that we run into trouble when we become too dependent on immediate rewards and lose focus on long-term goals. On some level, Bill was aware that he was acquiring too many things, but he had become so dependent on the rewards of acquiring that he had lost control.

⊷ Can You Resist Short-Term Payoffs?

Each statement describes how a person might feel when thinking about hoarding. Please indicate the extent to which you tend to agree or disagree with each statement. In each case, make your choice in terms of how you feel RIGHT NOW, not how you have felt in the past or would like to feel.

1. I should make sure that I don't feel bad.	TRUE	FALSE
2. I try to do what feels best to me at the moment.	TRUE	FALSE
3. I love the way it feels to find a treasure.	TRUE	FALSE
4. It's better to get what I can now, rather than wait for something better.	TRUE	FALSE

5. If I couldn't acquire treasures, I don't know how I would be able to feel good.	TRUE	FALSE
6. I should never feel anxious or sad.	TRUE	FALSE
7. If I passed up an opportunity, I'd be so upset that I wouldn't be able to get over it.	TRUE	FALSE
8. If I really want something, I should have it.	TRUE	FALSE

If you circled TRUE for *any* item on this measure, you might have a problem resisting short-term payoffs. If you circled TRUE for *more than one* item, then you are probably going to have to make substantial efforts to resist short-term payoffs and work toward a more patient approach to get the long-term payoff of beating hoarding.

So now you've met the five bad guys and have had a chance to determine how much of a role they play in your hoarding problems. If you didn't fill out the self-assessment tools, we encourage you to go back with a pencil and do so. Addressing these bad guys now, and taking a good hard look at them, will make you more likely to beat them as you go through this program. In the next chapter, we will introduce you to the "good guys" that will be on your side.

Meet the Good Guys
Strategies for Beating Hoarding

I n Chapter 4, we introduced you to the five bad guys that, in our experience, most frequently make it difficult for people to get their hoarding
problems under control. Everyone is a little bit different, and not everyone
experiences all five of the bad guys. If you did the self-assessment exercises
in the previous chapter, you have a sense of which bad guys are likely to
cause the biggest problems for you. If you haven't done so, we recommend
you go back and do them before you continue.

After reading about the bad guys, the prospect of tackling your hoarding problem might seem even more overwhelming. But before you get too
frustrated, read on: there are some "good guys" to help you along the way.
In this chapter, we will provide you with a basic outline of our program for
beating hoarding. We'll just introduce these good guys for now; later in the
book, we will talk about how to apply them in practice.

✳ The Basic Elements of the Program

This program consists of two primary elements: *non-acquiring* and *sorting*. Some people will do fine if they just work on sorting. However, if you
also have a problem of acquiring too many things
(e.g., you buy more than you need or pick up lots
of free things), you will also want to work on the
non-acquiring part of our program. For this part of
the program, we will ask you to actually go to the
places where you tend to acquire. If you usually buy things in particular

*This program consists of
two primary elements:
non-acquiring and sorting.*

stores, we will ask you to go to those stores; if you purchase things at yard sales, we will ask you to go to them; and so on. During these sessions you will challenge yourself by conducting experiments designed to help you think more clearly and to learn to tolerate urges to acquire without giving in to them. You'll also work on finding other activities that are fun for you and substitute for the enjoyment you get from acquiring.

If your home has a very large amount of clutter, you will want to spend a lot of time doing the sorting tasks. This will involve going through your possessions, a little bit at a time, and making decisions about what to do with them. The aim here is not simply to force yourself to throw things out, although we hope that this task will result in reduced clutter. Rather, think of sorting as a way to increase your understanding of why you save, to explore your beliefs about possessions, and to experiment with new beliefs and ways of doing things. In other words, the early goals of sorting include discovery and understanding, not just getting rid of things. During sorting tasks, you will work on two specific challenges: discarding the things you don't want to save, and organizing the things you do want to save.

As you go through the non-acquiring and sorting components of the program, the bad guys will most certainly show up. Here are the good guys, specific techniques to help you tip the balance in your favor.

Good Guy #1: Keeping Your Eyes on the Prize

As we discussed in Chapter 4, there are lots of obstacles to beating hoarding. Many of them keep you from spending the time needed to solve your hoarding problem. In Chapter 7 and elsewhere throughout the book, we will provide you with exercises to help you maintain a high level of awareness of the problem, keep your personal values and goals in mind, and find the strength to keep going. One thing we want to emphasize is that in the end, you want to be able to celebrate the things you own and use them to achieve your goals. This prize is worth keeping in mind.

Good Guy #2: Downward Arrow

The downward arrow is a strategy you can use to learn more about your beliefs, and to help you begin to challenge them. When you find yourself getting stuck, we'll ask you to identify what you think might happen. For each answer, you will keep asking more questions about what would be bad about that, and then what would be bad about *that,* until you get to the heart of your concern. For example, if you're feeling anxious about discarding something, you can ask yourself, "If I were to discard this, what's the worst that could happen?" *"I might need it someday."* "And what would be so bad about that?" *"If I need it and don't have it, then I'd really feel like an idiot."* "And how bad would that be for me to feel like an idiot?" And so forth. The aim of the downward arrow is to help you recognize what you are truly afraid of and what you truly believe about yourself. Understanding this enables you to evaluate how likely it is that the bad thing will happen and whether your beliefs seem reasonable or overblown. This is an important first step toward changing your thinking and your actions.

Good Guy #3: Thinking It Through

During sorting or non-acquisition tasks, we will ask you to think critically by talking your way through your decisions. For sorting, start by saying aloud all the thoughts you have about the possession in front of you. You may find that by doing so, your initial judgments about the value of the object will change. After you've done this a few times, keep track of the questions you raise about each possession. These questions will help speed up your decisions about saving. The questions people typically come up with include: "How many of these do I already have?" "How many would be enough?" "Do I have a specific plan to use this item within a reasonable timeframe?" "Have I used this in the past year?" "Is this of good quality?" "Do I really need it?" "Will discarding this help me solve my hoarding problem?"

Good Guy #4: Testing It Out

Sometimes, thinking-related strategies such as the downward arrow or thinking it through will not be enough. When you get to a puzzling issue or question that cannot be resolved through thinking alone, you will need to check it out. By that, we mean acting like a scientist who is studying hoarding by testing to see whether your thoughts are true, false, or partially true. First, it's critical to come up with specific predictions about what you think will happen. Predictions can be phrased as "if-then" statements, like "If I do *X*, then *Y* will happen." Here are some examples of hoarding-related predictions:

"If" statement	"Then" statement
If I don't buy this item... $\rightarrow$	...then I won't be able to stop thinking about it.

"If" statement	"Then" statement
If I throw away this item... $\rightarrow$	...then I'll feel terrible forever and won't be able to function.

Now, these predictions might be true, or they might not be true. How do you find out? As a scientist, your job will be to test your predictions. So, for example, if your prediction was "If I don't buy this item, then I won't be able to stop thinking about it," you need to try it out and watch carefully to see whether your prediction came true.

"If" statement	"Then" statement	Test
If I don't buy this item... $\rightarrow$	...then I won't be able to stop thinking about it. $\rightarrow$	I don't buy the item and pay attention to my thoughts over the next 24 hours.

"If" statement	"Then" statement	Test
If I throw away this item... $\rightarrow$	...then I'll feel terrible forever and won't be able to function. $\rightarrow$	I throw away the item and pay attention to my feelings and functioning over the next 24 hours.

Now check the outcome. Did your prediction come true?

"If" statement	"Then" statement	Test	Outcome
If I don't buy this item... $\rightarrow$	...then I won't be able to stop thinking about it. $\rightarrow$	I don't buy the item and pay attention to my thoughts over the next 24 hours. $\rightarrow$	After an hour I wasn't thinking about it as much, and by the next day I wasn't thinking about it at all.

"If" statement	"Then" statement	Test	Outcome
If I throw away this item... →	...then I'll feel terrible forever and won't be able to function. →	I throw away → the item and pay attention to my feelings and functioning over the next 24 hours.	When I threw it out, I only had minor feelings of anxiety. By that evening I felt fine. I was still able to function as I normally do.

If your prediction didn't come true, then revise your way of thinking by forming a new conclusion.

"If" statement	"Then" statement	Test	Outcome	Conclusion
If I don't buy this item... →	...then I won't be able to stop thinking about it. →	I don't buy → the item and pay attention to my thoughts over the next 24 hours.	After an hour → I wasn't thinking about it as much, and by the next day I wasn't thinking about it at all.	My brain doesn't just stay stuck on things forever. I am able to move on.

"If" statement	"Then" statement	Test	Outcome	Conclusion
If I throw away this item... →	...then I'll feel terrible forever and won't be able to function. →	I throw away → the item and pay attention to my feelings and function-ing over the next 24 hours.	When I threw it → out, I only had minor feelings of anxiety. By that evening I felt fine. I was still able to function as I normally do.	I'm more resilient than I thought. I can handle feeling bad, and can still function just fine. Even when I do feel bad, I won't feel that way forever.

So the bottom line for testing it out is to make a clear prediction, try doing the thing you're afraid of, and see whether the prediction comes true. If, after a long period of time, you still can't stop thinking about the item you didn't buy, or continue to feel terrible about the item you threw away and are really unable to function, then you'll know that your prediction was accurate. On the other hand, if you find yourself thinking less and less about it over time, or if you find yourself feeling and functioning OK, you might have to revise your original assumptions to take your new findings into account. Revising your thinking by testing it out is a powerful way to feel better and more in control.

Good Guy #5: Developing the Right Skills

Beating hoarding for good is not simply a question of throwing away clutter or stopping your acquisition. Certainly those are part of the solution, but some ways are better than others for getting you to your destination. For example, many people with hoarding problems have difficulty organizing their possessions. Things are often kept in a random or chaotic fashion, with important things mixed in with unimportant ones. It is often difficult to find things you need, and it's hard to know where to put things. Therefore, in this program you'll work on specific organizational strategies that will help you keep your possessions from getting out of control. Another skill we will work on involves taking a systematic approach to problem-solving, even for problems that do not directly involve clutter. Often, difficulty solving problems in living makes it hard for you to keep working on hoarding. Many of the people we've spoken to tell us about conflicts with family members, work problems, and other dilemmas that feel overwhelming and unsolvable. We will teach you a step-by-step strategy for addressing problems as they come up, so they are less likely to impede your progress.

Good Guy #6: Your Practice Muscle

To change longstanding behaviors like acquiring and saving, you will have to spend time practicing not acquiring, discarding, and organizing. That means managing your time to do the exercises in the book. Fitting this into their schedules can be a significant problem for people with hoarding difficulties. Luckily there is something you can do about it—PRACTICE. You can think of your ability to practice like a muscle that has not been exercised in a long time. You can't start out doing heavy lifting with that muscle. You have to begin with light weights and work your way up gradually. The first step in developing your Practice Muscle is to see how long you can spend working on this program right now. If you can spend half an hour a day on a consistent basis, you are at a good starting point. If you can spend only 5 minutes a day, you will need to work your way up. Don't despair, your Practice Muscle will get stronger. Start this week by spending 5 minutes with this book each day. Next week move it to 10 minutes. The third week, make it 15 minutes each day. Two things are key—"practice" every day and increase your time each week. Before you know it, you'll be up to an hour a day and making great progress.

How strong is your Practice Muscle? Rate how strong it is based on how many minutes you can work on hoarding each and every day.

Practice Muscle Strength

0	5	10	15	20	25	30	35	40	45	50	55	60

Minutes per day   Minutes per day

If your Practice Muscle Strength is 30 or above, you are in good shape to get started. Keep in mind that you may need to strengthen it more to make faster progress. If it is below 30, follow the instructions above to work your way up.

⁂ Will This Program Help Me?

Ultimately, you will get out of this program what you put into it. As we mentioned at the beginning of this book, the book by itself will not solve your hoarding problem. To succeed, you'll need to make a substantial investment of time, energy, and perhaps even some discomfort. But we think that this investment will pay off handsomely. No program can realistically promise to help everyone, and even those people who are helped by this program may still find that they continue to experience hoarding-related problems. As you know, getting control over clutter and hoarding is very hard. However, findings from our research studies tell us that it is possible. When we have studied these strategies in our Buried in Treasures Workshops using this book, up to 80 percent of participants rated themselves as "much improved" or "very much improved" after 3 to 4 months in the program.

⁂ Goals of the Program

What do you want to get out of this program? Different people have different answers to this question. Here are some of the most common goals that our clients have identified; the program in this book is specifically designed to accomplish these goals. Even more important, however, will be your personal goals, which will be addressed in Chapter 7.

1. *Understand why you hoard.* You have already begun to understand hoarding behaviors and the thoughts and feelings about possessions that influence these behaviors. We hope this program will promote optimism and feelings of empowerment, while decreasing the feelings of stigma, shame, and isolation that so many people with hoarding experience. A better understanding will increase your awareness of early warning signs for setbacks and your ability to manage them.

2. *Create living space you can use.* Most clients and their family members feel cramped by the clutter that prevents them from using their living spaces the way they want. Therefore, we will work on creating a healthy, happy living space. To achieve this goal, an early aim of the program will be to clear the most desired living spaces so you can use them in ways that suit your lifestyle and needs. For example, you will likely want to use kitchen counters for preparing meals, kitchen tables for eating meals, living rooms for relaxing personal and family activities and entertaining friends, playrooms for children's play activities, bedrooms for restful sleeping, and so forth. We will encourage you to focus immediately on the potential value of having these spaces uncluttered to help you stay motivated to keep them clutter-free.

3. *Find your things.* Improving your organizing skills adds a feeling of competency and self-esteem that helps you keep going. Developing a filing system and finding appropriate locations for storing saved items will enable you to find things quickly whenever you need them, and you will probably save money too.

4. *Improve your decision-making skills.* People with hoarding problems often have difficulty making decisions about their possessions and sometimes about other things too. This is often due to a fear of making mistakes and difficulty figuring out which features are most important to pay attention to. Practice making decisions using the strategies outlined in this book helps you feel more confident in your choices.

5. ***Reduce acquiring and enjoy other activities.*** This program will help you master strong urges to acquire new things you can't afford or don't have space or time to use effectively. Because acquiring is usually associated with strong positive emotions like comfort and joy, developing alternative pleasurable activities is also an important goal.

6. ***Reduce clutter.*** Parting with unneeded possessions is what many people with hoarding problems fear most, but it is clutter that causes the most problem. As the goals of creating living space by organizing and reducing acquiring are accomplished, the volume of possessions will gradually diminish, although you will still need to remove clutter by recycling, giving away, selling, or discarding items. Removing items will become much easier after you have established personal rules for keeping and storing desired items.

As you pursue these goals, you will also learn problem-solving skills that enable you to resolve a variety of problems that can arise that threaten your progress. These skills can be applied to all kinds of situations, such as family conflicts about hoarding, how to make space for sorting, managing money to avoid overspending, and so forth. Once you have gotten the clutter under control, you will also gain new habits that prevent the re-accumulation of clutter. You will learn to notice early warning signs for hoarding-related problems so you can use your skills. In addition, as work on hoarding occupies less of your time, other fun or productive activities should replace time spent on hoarding.

Fact File for Family and Friends
Instructions for Coaches

Overcoming hoarding is difficult. Many people find it helpful to have a support person or "coach" who can assist them with the process. As a coach, you will work together with the person with the hoarding problem. Here are some ways to make your involvement most helpful:

Meet as a team with the person with the hoarding problem. Two people working together is a recipe for success, whereas two people working in different directions will not work.

Help the person remain focused on the task in front of him or her. People with hoarding problems often find themselves easily distracted, especially when they are trying to reduce clutter, make decisions about possessions, or resist the urge to acquire things. The coach can be very helpful by politely reminding the person what he or she is supposed to be doing right now.

Provide emotional support. In our experience, acting like a taskmaster or drill sergeant just makes people feel nervous or angry and interferes with their ability to learn new approaches. They feel even more isolated and misunderstood, and retreat into bad habits. Therefore, we suggest using a gentle touch. It's often very helpful to express empathy with statements such as, "I can see how hard this is for you," or "I understand that you have mixed feelings about whether to tackle this clutter." The person with the hoarding problem is going through some major stress and often needs a sympathetic ear or even a shoulder to cry on.

Visit them in their home. One of the most powerful things you can do is to visit the home of your loved one without talking about hoarding. Visitors increase motivation to work on hoarding and help jumpstart the process of using the home for normal activities.

Help the person make decisions, but DO NOT make decisions for him or her. During treatment, the person with the hoarding problem is learning to develop new rules for deciding what to keep and what to remove. It will help them to have you listen while they describe their thoughts about items they are considering discarding. You needn't say much; let them think through each item and come to a conclusion. Their job is to develop these skills; yours is to listen while they do so.

Be a cheerleader. Sometimes, we all need an extra boost when things get difficult. Calling to remind them of a homework assignment, telling them you believe they can do it, and noticing when they are doing a good job are all good cheerleading strategies.

Help with hauling. Many people who hoard have accumulated so much clutter that it would take them a year or more to discard it all by themselves. This makes it easy to get discouraged because progress is slow. Coaches are very helpful when they roll up their sleeves and help remove items from the home, provided that the person with the hoarding problem makes all the decisions and remains fully in charge of the process.

Accompany the person on non-acquiring trips. People who acquire too many things will need to practice going to a tempting store or yard sale and not buying anything. It can be extremely helpful to have someone go along to help them resist temptation and make the trip a success.

Even the most well-meaning coaches can make themselves less helpful by using the wrong strategies. Here are some DON'Ts:

Don't argue with the person about what to get rid of and what to acquire. Debates about the

(continued)

usefulness of an item or the need to get rid of it will only produce negative emotional reactions that don't facilitate progress. Instead, whenever you feel the conflict, take a break, relax a bit, and remind yourself how difficult this is for the person with the hoarding problem. You can always come back to it later.

Don't take over decisions. It would certainly be easier and quicker if coaches simply took charge, decided what should stay and what should go, and hauled the clutter out themselves. But this method doesn't teach people how to manage their problem: the clutter will just build up again. Instead, be sure the person with the hoarding problem is in charge at all times and makes all decisions.

Don't touch or move anything without permission. Imagine how you would feel if a well-meaning person came into your home and handled your things without permission. Doing this can damage the trust between you and make it impossible for the person to proceed.

Don't tell the person how he or she should feel. It can be very hard to understand why someone feels so sentimental about keeping what looks like trash to you or feels afraid to get rid of something that is clearly useless. But these feelings developed for reasons that are not always clear. Be as patient as you can. We know that coaching can be frustrating.

Don't work beyond your own tolerance level. To be a good coach, you have to take care of yourself first and then help your friend or family member. So feel free to set limits on how long and how much work you can do on any given occasion. Pat yourself on the back for your own efforts; helping someone who hoards is very hard work.

6

How Did This Happen?

Before we start to tackle the hoarding problem, let's discuss what we know about how hoarding develops. This will accomplish two important things. First, it will help you understand hoarding for what it is—a problem of emotional, mental, behavioral, and social well-being. Second, it will give some important clues to how to beat the problem. Knowledge is power—the more you know, the better equipped you will be to work toward improving things. Therefore, we recommend

Hoarding is a problem of emotional, mental, behavioral, and social well-being.

you read this chapter completely. In fact, you'll probably want to read it more than once in order to really get how your hoarding problem works. In our Buried in Treasures Workshops, some people felt that once they understood the material in this chapter, they felt much more able to get control of the problem.

Let's start by defining hoarding as a *mental health problem*. We realize that these words might be hard for some people to swallow. For some, the words conjure up very unpleasant (maybe even scary) images of serious mental illnesses such as schizophrenia. Some people with hoarding do have these kinds of problems, but most don't and won't. We don't mean in any way to imply that having a mental health problem means that you are "crazy," "damaged," or a "hopeless case." Quite the contrary: many people with hoarding are smart, witty, and delightful, even though we are well aware that they are suffering. What we *do* mean is that people with hoarding are not fully in control of their behavior. They didn't sign up for this. They are hooked into a pattern of behavior that even they cannot fully understand or manage. If you are a person with hoarding, perhaps someone has told you that your hoarding is due to laziness, personality flaws, or stubbornness. By defining hoarding as a mental health problem, we hope it is clear that we don't agree with these opinions. But at the same time, having a mental health problem does not mean you are off the hook. Hoarding is *your* problem, even if it is not your *fault*, and only you can fix it. By now you understand that our goal is to help you do just that.

There's another important issue with this definition. In many cases, family members, friends, or outside agencies have tried to help by clearing out things from the person's home. Sometimes this is done with the person's permission and sometimes not. We think that these kinds of interventions miss the point. When we focus all of our efforts on the person's house—for example, if we send the person on vacation and then clean out the house while he or she is away, we're treating hoarding as a *house problem*. But hoarding is not just a house problem; it's also a *person problem*. Unless the person makes fundamental, sustainable changes in how he or she thinks, feels, and acts—that is, alters the way he or she relates to possessions—the problem is still there. This is exactly what research tells us: when someone else takes over the discarding process, the person with the hoarding problem usually continues to acquire and save items, and the house fills up again—sometimes more so than before the clean-out.

Hoarding is not just a house problem; it's also a person problem.

So throughout this book, you'll notice that we spend a lot less time talking about your house and a lot more time talking about you—how you feel, how you think, and what you do. From our research and our experience talking with people with hoarding, we think that much of the problem can be attributed to issues in your brain, in your thoughts, in your emotions, and in your behavior.

✳ Hoarding in Your Brain

Findings From Brain Scans

Some researchers have used brain scans to try to understand what's going on in the brains of people who hoard. We're going to skip some of the dry details, but there are a couple of things you should know. We asked people with and without Hoarding Disorder who agreed to participate in our study to bring in a bag of "junk" mail from their homes. While they were in a functional magnetic resonance imaging (fMRI) scanner, they were shown each piece of mail and asked to decide whether to keep it or discard it. In addition, people in the study had to make some other decisions that had nothing to do with their own possessions, while still in the scanner. When we looked at the results of the brain scans, we saw that the brain activity of people with hoarding disorder differed from that of people without hoarding in two important ways. First, when they were making relatively unimportant decisions (unrelated to their own possessions), parts of the frontal and temporal lobes of the brain were underactive in people with hoarding disorder. These parts of the brain are involved with judging the relevance or importance of things. On the other hand, when they had to make decisions about whether to keep or discard their own possessions, these same regions of the brain were overactive in people with Hoarding Disorder. The brain activity had flip-flopped from too low to too high.

What does it mean when these areas of the brain are not active enough? We suspect that it means that some people with Hoarding Disorder consider many things unimportant or irrelevant. Many family members of people who hoard get frustrated with their loved ones, asking, "How can they stand to live like this? Don't they see how awful their living conditions are?" Well, our brain scans suggest that perhaps they don't see it, or at least they don't perceive it in the same way as people without Hoarding Disorder do. "Clean freaks" can't walk by a pile of clutter without reacting to it emotionally. It bothers them, and they feel a need to do something about it. In brain language, their frontal and temporal lobes are telling them, "Hey, this is important and you'd better pay attention to it!" But if you have Hoarding Disorder, your brain might not be sending you the same message.

But then there's the flip-flop. When they have to make a real decision about their own possessions, people who hoard show overactivity in these same frontal and temporal regions. What does it mean when these areas of the brain are too active? If these parts of the brain are responsible for telling you, "Hey, this is important and you'd better pay attention to it!," imagine now that this message is being screamed at you while you're trying to make a decision. Here, too, many people have a hard time understanding why people who hoard would have a hard time with such "simple" decisions. But when we understand how the person's brain is working, we see it's not so simple. Everything feels important, relevant, and worthy of attention. And when everything is important, then nothing can be thrown away.

Does this mean you're doomed? Absolutely not. Sigmund Freud once famously remarked, "Biology is not destiny." Yes, your brain activity can exert powerful influences over your thinking, your emotions, and your behavior. But it can go the other way as well: by working on how you think, how you feel, and how you act, you can make positive changes to how your brain functions. In fact, our research shows us exactly that: when people have a good response to cognitive-behavioral therapy (the strategies outlined in this book), their brain activity becomes more normal. Change your mind, and you change your brain.

Problems With Attention

Many people with hoarding problems experience great difficulty sustaining attention to tasks. They find themselves becoming easily distracted by things going on around them or by their own thoughts or feelings. Some of the people we've treated have been diagnosed with attention-deficit/hyperactivity disorder (ADHD), which is a chronic problem with maintaining attention and focus. Other people don't have ADHD but find that their concentration is impaired by depression, fatigue, anxiety, or the sheer number of things they have to think about. Attention—the ability to filter out distractions—is one of the most basic cognitive functions; without it, even the simplest of tasks can become extremely difficult. As we're writing this book, we've had to remove ourselves from distractions—turn off the TV or radio, take the phone off the hook, and retreat to the seclusion of our offices. The more things that are happening around us, the less efficiently we work. Maybe you've noticed the same process in your own work. For people with hoarding, the distractions are more frequent, more intense, and more compelling—and often they come from inside, rather than outside, the person. Imagine trying to do something very complicated, like a difficult math problem or crossword puzzle, in the midst of a buffalo stampede. You'd probably find the task extremely difficult and taxing, and it would likely overwhelm your cognitive capacity. That's what it's like for some people with hoarding to try to sort their possessions. Even though they try to focus on sorting, they perceive too many external demands that take them off task, and new thoughts keep coming up that seem immediately important—the darn buffalo keep getting in the way!

While there are problems maintaining attention during the unpleasant tasks of sorting and discarding, a seemingly opposite problem often occurs during acquisition. When people who compulsively buy or pick up free things "lock on" to an item they want to obtain, they can't stop thinking about it. Their attention is focused so narrowly on the object and all the opportunities it could provide them, they can't see what it will truly cost them in money, space, time, or trouble—until they get home.

Problems With Categorization

Imagine that you are seated at a big table, looking at a big pile of your possessions. There's a lot of stuff here, with no particular rhyme or reason: some clothing, some cans of food, some magazines, and so on. Someone asks you to sort the items but doesn't give you any more instruction than that. What kinds of categories would you create? How many piles would there be? If you're like most people who don't have hoarding problems, you would probably come up with a relatively small number of categories—for example, food, reading material, clothing—and each category would contain a large number of items. If, on the other hand, you are like a lot of people with hoarding problems, your categories would be different. You might come up with a much larger number of categories—for example, instead of "food," you might have vegetables, fruits, tuna fish, oatmeal, condiments, and so on—and each category would contain a small number of items. This is exactly what we found in one of our research studies. Compared to people without hoarding problems, people who hoard seem to have a difficult time putting their possessions into big categories. It's as if each item is so special that it can't be categorized with other items. The result is a lot of little categories rather than a few big ones.

People who hoard seem to have a difficult time putting their possessions into big categories.

Interestingly, this phenomenon occurred only when people had to sort their own possessions: when sorting other people's things, they had no difficulty. This suggests that people with hoarding don't have a general problem categorizing things, but when dealing with their own possessions, their emotions get in the way and cause them to process information differently. When you are trying to accomplish tasks such as cleaning up your home, it's much easier to work with a smaller number of categories. If you're working with just one category of "food," for example, it's much easier to deduce that everything from this category belongs in the kitchen. If, on the other hand, you have 8, 9, or 10 different food-related categories, you then have to consider and make decisions about each one. What would have been a relatively straightforward decision now becomes a complicated series of decisions.

Problems With Decision-Making

Given the problems with categorizing and attention described above, perhaps it's no surprise that people with hoarding problems also frequently have a hard time making decisions. Sometimes decision-making problems show up only when trying to decide what to keep and what to discard. However, for many people, indecisiveness plagues them throughout the day, in virtually everything they do. They can't decide what to wear, where to go, what to eat, and so forth. For these people, even everyday decisions feel like a major ordeal. Sometimes, indecisiveness is related to beliefs, such as perfectionism (which we will talk about in more detail below). At other times, indecisiveness seems to be due to difficulty processing all of the information needed to make a decision.

When we talked to Helen (from Chapter 2) about her clutter, it became clear that she had substantial problems making decisions. She told us, "When a piece of mail comes in, I just don't know what to do with it. Is it important? Is it trash? If I throw it away, will it turn out that I needed it? What if I make the wrong decision? I get anxious and I just don't know what to do, so I put it down and leave it for later."

Problems With Memory

Many people who hoard tell us they have trouble remembering things. They don't remember chores they must do, bills they must pay, appointments they must keep, and so on. These people often use physical objects as a visual reminder. For example, many people (with and without hoarding problems) leave a bill out someplace visible so that they will remember to pay it. We do that, too, sometimes. It can be an effective memory aid. The problem comes when we have too many visual reminders in front of us, especially when they are not organized in an efficient manner. Imagine, for example, that instead of one bill that needs to be paid, we have 10—and instead of leaving them in one pile, we leave them in various places around the house. We're also out of milk, so we leave the empty milk carton on top of a pile of newspapers. And we need to return that sweater that didn't fit to the store, so we leave it on the couch, on top of some of the bills. Pretty soon, it's easy to see how our strategy for facilitating memory has backfired and become self-defeating: instead of remembering all of these things efficiently, we now become overwhelmed and confused and are actually *less* likely to remember them.

Hoarding in Your Thoughts

In many ways, the beliefs and thoughts of people with hoarding problems aren't terribly different from those of people without hoarding problems. When faced with difficult decisions about what to keep and what to discard, or what to acquire and what to leave, it's quite natural for people (including the authors of this book!) to struggle with thoughts like:

> "This might be useful."
> "I don't want to make the wrong decision."
> "This item has sentimental value to me."
> "This item is part of my identity."
> "This item gives me a sense of security."

So the issue for most people who hoard is not that their thoughts and beliefs are completely irrational. Rather, the problem is that these thoughts and beliefs have become so entrenched and inflexible that they get in the way of making wise choices. The person has gotten out of the habit of thinking flexibly, seeing things from more than one perspective. Below, we'll describe some common beliefs that are problematic for people with hoarding.

Beliefs About Usefulness, Waste, and Responsibility

As we described above, many people with hoarding are very good at thinking of ways to use items. Where other people see trash, they see opportunity. Some items, for example, have not been completely used up, such as a box of cereal that still has a few stale flakes in it. Other items might be reusable, like used paper towel rolls that might be useful for crafts. Still other items could be recycled or given away.

This line of thinking can be tricky. On one hand, the person is trying to be frugal, creative, or environmentally conscious—all of which are virtues.

But people's strengths can also become their limitations. Taken too far, these virtuous ways of thinking become rigid and untenable. Instead of helping the person live well, the thoughts become insurmountable roadblocks. The thinking goes something like this: "I can think of some ways to reuse this item. Therefore, I am *responsible* for doing so, and if I fail to do so I am being *wasteful*. If I am wasteful, I will be a *lousy person*. But right now, I'm tired and stressed and I don't have enough time, so I can't actually follow through with this plan. So, to avoid being a lousy person, I will hold onto this item until I can deal with it." But that time almost never comes.

Overly Creative Thinking

Many of the people we have met with hoarding problems are highly intelligent, clever, and creative people. Believe it or not, we think that sometimes this is part of the problem. When a person who hoards holds an item in his or her hands, all kinds of wonderful ideas and opportunities come to mind: "I bet I could fix this up!" "I know just who would want this!" "I could take this apart and use the parts for something else!" "I could turn this around and sell it for a profit!" "I could reuse this and help the environment!" "I could make all kinds of crafts or decorations from this!"

Sound familiar? If so, you may be one of these highly creative people who runs into trouble. Because your brain can come up with so many great ideas, you become much more reluctant to part with objects. In many cases, the problem is that the person's creativity exceeds his or her physical capacity to carry out the plans—the brain writes checks that the body can't cash. It's great when a person comes up with an idea for an item and carries out that plan, and then comes up with another idea for a different item and carries out that plan. This is typical for the average handyperson, entrepreneur, gift-giver, or craftsperson. But people who hoard often come up with idea after idea, saving things for all kinds of creative reasons but never following through with those plans. They have become victims of their own clever minds.

Perfectionism

It's hard for many people to understand how perfectionism and hoarding can go together. After all, when most of us think of a "perfectionist," we think of someone whose home is immaculate, with everything in its place.

But for some people, perfectionism works in a different way. They become so afraid of making the wrong decision—for example, that they will accidentally throw away something useful—that the prospect of making decisions gives rise to strong feelings of anxiety and worry. As a result, the person tends to avoid the decision-making process altogether. The basic operating principle seems to be, "If I can't be sure of doing it exactly right, I'd better not do it at all." Paradoxically, therefore, the person's perfectionistic beliefs contribute to his or her home becoming the model of *im*perfection.

Hoarding in Your Emotions

Feeling Rotten

Most (though not all) of the people we've met with hoarding problems are unhappy. Sometimes they're unhappy about the hoarding problem itself, sometimes not. But they are usually unhappy about something, even if they can't quite put their finger on what that something is. One kind of emotional discomfort we often see in people who hoard is *sadness, grief, loneliness, or longing*. Sometimes that means that the person feels persistently sad or depressed (as we've mentioned, in our research we've found that many people who hoard also have clinical depression). Other times those feelings come and go, showing up only in certain circumstances (like when parting with possessions). Another kind of emotional discomfort is *anxiety, fear, tension, or worry*. Lots of people who hoard also have a clinical anxiety disorder, but even those who don't might still describe feeling tense or nervous, especially when they have to make decisions they aren't sure about. Still other forms of upsetting emotions are *guilt and regret*, emotions that often arise when the person who hoards believes he or she is responsible for objects or people who might need them. Some people also experience *anger, frustration, irritability, or annoyance*. These feelings can really show up when it seems like someone else is trying to control you and your stuff. Angry and hurt feelings make it hard to listen to the opinions of others without being defensive.

How do these feelings relate to hoarding? Often, when we feel rotten, we feel a strong motivation to do something to feel better. We'll talk about this issue later in this chapter, but the short version is, a lot of acquiring and saving behaviors are attempts to get immediate relief from unpleasant feelings.

Sentimental Attachment

People who hoard frequently experience strong feelings toward their possessions, as well as strong beliefs about their value or importance. One of these reactions is a strong sense of emotional attachment to possessions. Most of us feel some attachment to some things. We keep an old pair of jeans we've had for years that are broken in just right, or a photo album containing cherished pictures of loved ones, or mementos from special occasions in our lives. This kind of sentimentality is natural and helps us feel connected to other people and other times. People who hoard, however, often feel this kind of sentimental attachment to things that most others wouldn't: a grocery list, a single sock, clothing that no longer fits, and so forth. For some people, these items serve as a tangible record of their lives; throwing them away feels like losing that part of their lives. Some people's homes are cluttered with items that once belonged to a loved one who has died, or that remind them of their loved one. In their grief, they keep these things because getting rid of them feels like discarding the good memories of that person. Again, this is not necessarily unusual; many of us hold on to things that remind us of people we love and miss. But some people keep so many things that rather than creating good memories or honoring their loved ones, they create problems for themselves.

A rather extreme version of attachment happens when we start to think or act as if our possessions are like people—giving objects thoughts, feelings, desires, and so on. Psychologists call this "anthropomorphism"—believing that inanimate objects have human-like traits. We've seen several examples of this phenomenon in our clinical and research programs. One client was reluctant to throw away an old puppet because she thought it would be "sad." Another felt so bad after throwing away an empty yogurt container that she wanted to apologize to it for not giving it a good home. These people were not delusional. Rationally, they were perfectly aware that the puppet and the yogurt container were inanimate objects that didn't have emotions. But they couldn't shake those nagging feelings of sadness, empathy, and guilt and felt compelled to act accordingly.

Feelings of Identity

For other people, the items give them a sense of self, as if they are defined by what they own. One woman who felt this way told us, "If I throw too much away, there will be nothing left of me." We might call this kind of thinking "object-identity fusion." We have met lots of people whose possessions serve to help them define who they would like to be. Some think of themselves as a craftsperson or an artist but spend more time acquiring new supplies than actually making any crafts or art. Others view themselves as generous gift-givers or clever carpenters or engineers who can fix things—but if they buy gifts and don't give them away or if they collect broken chairs or lawn mowers and never fix them, they are not who they aspire to be.

Here's what Bill had to say about his acquiring and saving: "I have a good sense of the value of things, and I can spot a bargain. I was at a flea market last weekend and picked up some stereo speakers on sale for $5, and I know I've seen those same speakers selling elsewhere for $15." Bill thinks of himself as a shrewd investor. This is his identity. The problem, though, is that Bill rarely sells the things he buys. Instead, they pile up in his home collecting dust. What we think is happening here is that when he sees a bargain, Bill experiences himself as the person he wants to be (a shrewd investor). And while he is focusing on his new acquisition, he is (at least in his mind). This image is highly reinforcing, and whenever he looks at one of the things he has collected he sees himself the way he wants to be. That image would be painful to give up by not acquiring the speakers he knows are a bargain. That would feel like giving up on his identity. In a sense, Bill is defining himself by what he *has,* rather than what he *does.*

Feelings of Safety, Security, and Control

Some people save possessions because they derive a feeling of safety or security from them. We have met people who described their possessions as a "nest" or "cocoon" that makes them feel protected from what they perceive to be a dangerous world. Sometimes people worry that something bad will happen if they are not surrounded with their possessions. In other cases, however, people know their possessions aren't actually protecting them, but they still get an emotional feeling of security. The irony, of course, is that in many cases the person's possessions increase, rather than decrease, the risk of harm. High levels of clutter can put the person at risk of fire, falling, and disease—not to mention a reduced quality of life.

When people derive feelings of safety and security from their possessions, it can feel intolerable whenever someone touches them or attempts to remove them. Even if the other person is trying to help, the person who hoards feels as if his or her fundamental security is being threatened. Therefore, some people develop a strong need to maintain control over their possessions at all times. This problem can be compounded when well-meaning family members move or discard items without the person's knowledge. When the person discovers this, he or she often feels violated and threatened and responds with an even stronger need for control.

Positive Feelings

In addition to the feelings we have just described, many people with hoarding experience strong positive feelings—excitement, joy, wonder, pleasure—when they see new things they'd like to acquire or find things they had forgotten about. Many women with hoarding describe feeling intense excitement when they go shopping and often spend more than they planned because of feelings of intense pleasure. Many people also report feeling great joy when they discover a lost item that turns up in a pile they are rummaging through to find something else. Unfortunately, these positive feelings can get in the way of rational thinking about the costs of acquiring and hoarding, as you will see shortly.

❋ Hoarding in Your Behavior

Ultimately, the causes of clutter are behavioral: acquiring too much and not parting with enough. But why do people behave this way? For many people, their possessions evoke strong moods—some pleasant, some unpleasant. These moods, in turn, become powerful motivators. As we have described earlier, many people find that the prospect of discarding a possession leads to feelings of anxiety or fear. Others report experiencing grief, loss, sadness, or guilt when they think about letting go of a possession. Frustration and anger often erupt when a person thinks about sorting and discarding, especially if he or she feels pressured by others to do so. So, of course, the person tries to escape or avoid those uncomfortable feelings by not sorting (or perhaps even looking at) his or her possessions, by keeping an item rather than making the difficult decision to discard it, or by acquiring something to make himself or herself feel better. The person is using avoidance or acquiring as a way to get *relief* from feeling bad.

On the positive side, many people report a good or "high" feeling when they look at a possession, or find something they had lost, or find a "treasure" they want to acquire. They feel such a strong pull toward the pleasure (we will call this a *payoff*) that they end up doing things that ultimately aren't in their best interest—for example, buying something that they cannot afford and keeping things they might otherwise discard.

In many cases, therefore, we can think of the person's clutter as an external means of mood control: the person uses possessions to maximize the good feelings (payoffs) while minimizing the bad feelings (relief). Of course, this does not always work out in the person's best interest, such as when clutter swells to the point of being unbearable.

Bill is a great example of someone whose actions are being controlled, in part, by payoffs. When Bill goes to a flea market and finds a bargain, he feels a sense of delight. He congratulates himself on finding this "treasure" and experiences what he calls "the thrill of victory." It's easy to see how this good feeling can be a powerful motivator: he's likely to keep going back again and again in search of that feeling. Of course, the feeling never lasts long. When Bill gets home with his new possession, he quickly realizes he has no place to put it. Frustrated and confused, he tosses it on top of the pile and eventually forgets about it. You might ask, why don't Bill's feelings of frustration, confusion, and unhappiness with the clutter in his home serve as deterrents to acquiring more things? For the same reason that hangovers are not powerful deterrents for people with drinking problems. We all tend to be motivated most strongly by immediate rather than delayed consequences. This is a big part of the problem: instead of being able to step back and appreciate the long-term consequences of our actions, we become slaves to the here and now.

Helen's situation is a little different. She doesn't report a thrill or good feeling that comes from acquiring possessions. Rather, she is a victim of relief: her actions serve to protect her from bad feelings. As we have already learned, when Helen handles a piece of junk mail, all kinds of worries come into her mind. She fears that she will make the wrong decision, that she will need it later, and so forth. She also experiences powerful negative feelings of anxiety and being overwhelmed. It is these feelings that exert the strongest influence over Helen's behavior. By avoiding discarding, she doesn't have to experience those strong negative feelings or scary thoughts. Of course, she also accumulates a great deal of clutter, and you might well ask why the condition of her house doesn't motivate her to start cleaning. The answer is the same as it was for Bill: long-term consequences, unpleasant as they may be, simply are not very powerful motivators compared to the immediate thrill of acquiring or the relief of avoiding the confusing and scary task of discarding.

✳ An Experiment for You to Try

We'd like to help you get a better sense of why you save things. For this experiment, we want you to select three items from your home (or wherever the clutter is), and see if you can part with them (by discarding, recycling, selling, or donating them). Our goal here is not to have you just start throwing stuff out; rather, this is a good time for you to learn something about yourself and your reasons for saving. At the end of the experiment you might decide to part with the items, or you might not; that's completely up to you.

To start, go choose three possessions. One of them should be something you expect will be *easy* to discard, one should be something you think will be *moderately difficult* to discard, and one should be something you would find *quite difficult* to discard.

Start with the easy item first. Right now, challenge yourself to go put it in the wastebasket, the recycle bin, or a donation box—that is, try your best to part with it. Use the form below to describe what happens.

━◆ Easy Item

What is the item? _____

Check the box next to any of the following you experienced. For anything you checked, please add whatever comments you think would be helpful.

☐ I had difficulty keeping my attention on task.

_____

☐ I had difficulty deciding what category it fit into.

_____

☐ I had a hard time making a decision.

_____

☐ I thought of more and more reasons to keep it.

_____

☐ I felt like I needed to keep it to help my memory.

_____

☐ I was concerned about being wasteful or irresponsible.

_____

☐ I was worried about making a mistake or being imperfect.

_____

☐ I felt sentimentally or emotionally attached to the item.

_____

☐ I felt like the item was part of who I am.

_____

☐ It felt unsafe or out of control to part with the item.

_____

☐ It felt too uncomfortable or difficult to part with the item.

_____

☐ Other

_____

On a scale from 0–10, how difficult was it to part with the item?

0	1	2	3	4	5	6	7	8	9	10
Extremely Easy		Pretty Easy		Moderately Difficult				Pretty Difficult		Extremely Difficult

Did you actually part with the item? _____ Yes _____ No

Next, try it with the item that you think would be _moderately difficult_ to discard. We want you to try this whether or not you parted with the easier item. Remember, the goal is to learn about your saving, not just to have you throw stuff out. Take the moderately difficult item and try your best to part with it. Use the form below to describe what happens.

What is the item? _____

Check the box next to any of the following you experienced. For anything you checked, please add whatever comments you think would be helpful.

☐ I had difficulty keeping my attention on task.

_____

☐ I had difficulty deciding what category it fit into.

_____

☐ I had a hard time making a decision.

_____

☐ I thought of more and more reasons to keep it.

_____

☐ I felt like I needed to keep it to help my memory.

_____

☐ I was concerned about being wasteful or irresponsible.

_____

☐ I was worried about making a mistake or being imperfect.

_____

☐ I felt sentimentally or emotionally attached to the item.

_____

☐ I felt like the item was part of who I am.

_____

☐ It felt unsafe or out of control to part with the item.

_____

☐ It felt too uncomfortable or difficult to part with the item.

_____

☐ Other

_____

On a scale from 0–10, how difficult was it to part with the item?

0	1	2	3	4	5	6	7	8	9	10

Extremely   Pretty Easy   Moderately Difficult   Pretty   Extremely
Easy   Difficult   Difficult

Did you actually part with the item? _____ Yes _____ No

Finally, try it with the item that you think would be *quite difficult* to discard, whether or not you parted with the two previous items. Take the quite difficult item and try your best to part with it. Use the form below to describe what happens.

⌗ Quite Difficult Item

What is the item? _____

Check the box next to any of the following you experienced. For anything you checked, please add whatever comments you think would be helpful.

☐ I had difficulty keeping my attention on task.

_____

☐ I had difficulty deciding what category it fit into.

_____

☐ I had a hard time making a decision.

_____

☐ I thought of more and more reasons to keep it.

_____

☐ I felt like I needed to keep it to help my memory.

_____

☐ I was concerned about being wasteful or irresponsible.

_____

☐ I was worried about making a mistake or being imperfect.

_____

☐ I felt sentimentally or emotionally attached to the item.

_____

☐ I felt like the item was part of who I am.

_____

☐ It felt unsafe or out of control to part with the item.

_____

☐ It felt too uncomfortable or difficult to part with the item.

_____

☐ Other

_____

On a scale from 0–10, how difficult was it to part with the item?

0	1	2	3	4	5	6	7	8	9	10
Extremely Easy		Pretty Easy		Moderately Difficult				Pretty Difficult		Extremely Difficult

Did you actually part with the item? _____ Yes _____ No

Pause for just a moment and reflect on what kind of things you noticed. What kind of reasons did you have for saving? (Check all that apply to you)

☐ I have problems sustaining attention.

☐ I have problems with categorization.

☐ I have problems with decision-making.

☐ I engage in overly creative thinking.

☐ I have poor confidence in my memory.

☐ I have strong beliefs about usefulness, waste, or responsibility.

☐ I have fears of mistakes or imperfection.

☐ I have a strong emotional attachment to items.

☐ I use possessions to feel a sense of identity.

☐ I have strong beliefs about safety, security, or the need to control my possessions.

☐ I avoid discarding because it feels bad.

☐ Other

✳ Putting It All Together

As you can see, hoarding is a complex phenomenon that can be very different from one person to the next. Although all hoarding is characterized by the physical presence of clutter, the *reasons* for clutter can be very different. Understanding your reasons for clutter will be an important first step.

In Figure 6.1, you can see a visual depiction of the reasons for hoarding we've outlined in this chapter. On the right side of the figure is clutter. Moving to the left, we see that clutter is the direct result of specific behavior patterns such as acquiring or avoiding discarding. The behavior patterns, in turn, are caused by emotional attachment and unhelpful beliefs about possessions, problems processing information, and relief or payoffs.

Understanding your reasons for clutter will be an important first step.

Let's take a look at how the reasons for hoarding can be different for different people. In Figure 6.2, we've diagrammed Helen's hoarding problems at the top and Bill's hoarding problems at the bottom. As you can see, Helen and Bill are similar in some ways and dissimilar in others. Both have an excessive amount of clutter in their living space and tend to avoid

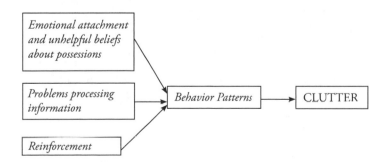

Figure 6.1 A Diagram of Why People Hoard.

discarding (behavior patterns). Each also uses avoidance as a way of preventing bad feelings. However, Helen's beliefs about possessions are more often about perfectionism and making mistakes (strong worries that she will make the wrong decision), whereas Bill's beliefs involve a sense of identity derived from his possessions (his possessions help him to think of himself as an entrepreneur and finder of lost treasures). Helen's information-processing problems include difficulty making decisions and sustaining attention, whereas Bill is a victim of his own "over-creativity." Finally, Bill, but not Helen, derives positive feelings when he acquires new possessions.

People with hoarding problems also frequently experience difficulty making decisions.

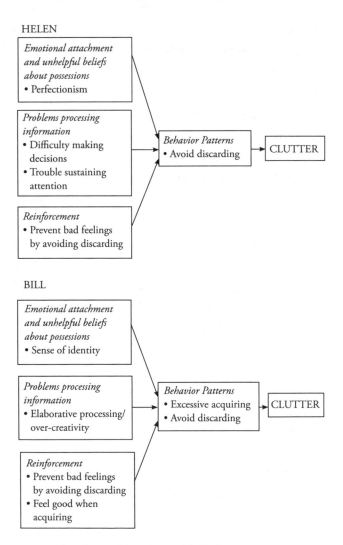

Figure 6.2 Helen and Bill's Diagrams.

Now we'd like you to try it. Figure 6.3 is a blank visual depiction of hoarding for you to write in. As is the case throughout this book, we think you will get the best results if you actually go get a pencil or pen and write in the book; just thinking about it won't be enough. Use Figure 6.3 to see if you can identify your reasons for hoarding. Don't worry about doing it perfectly; you can always go back and modify what you've written. But don't skip this part—the ideas you generate here will become part of the foundation for your program for getting control over your hoarding.

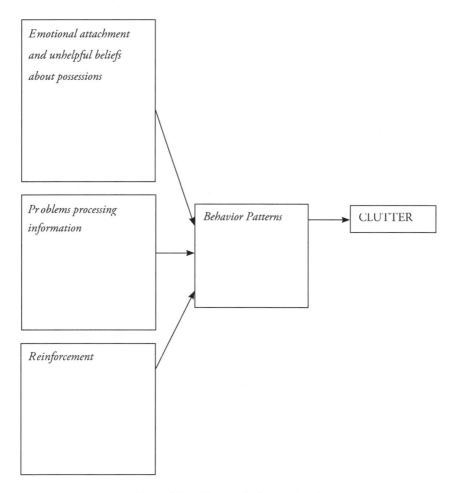

Figure 6.3 A Diagram for You to Complete.

7

Enhancing Motivation

❋ Motivational Boost

Motivation is a tricky thing. Sometimes, when we notice a problem, we feel highly motivated to do something about it right away. We identify it immediately as being something we want to work on, we know just what to do about it, and we feel confident in our ability to do so. But this is not always how we feel. We might not think something is a problem, or perhaps not a particularly high-priority problem. Or we might recognize that it's a problem, but not know what to do about it. Or perhaps, even if we know what to do about it, we don't think we can actually pull it off. Sometimes, even with the best intentions, other things come up to distract us, such as fatigue, other stressors, or other priorities. Just to make things more complicated, our level of motivation may change from day to day or even moment to moment: we're really committed to working on something one day but feel ambivalent the next.

The aim of this chapter is to give you a good motivational shot in the arm. Even if you're feeling very motivated right now to work on your hoarding problem, we still recommend you read this chapter. Why? Because even the most highly motivated person will eventually reach a point where his or her motivation wavers. When that happens (notice we didn't say "if"), we want you to have some good ideas in mind to keep you going.

Even the most highly motivated person will eventually reach a point where his or her motivation wavers.

✳ **Recognizing the Problem**

How accurate is your perception of the severity of the hoarding problem? One way of answering this question is to compare how you think about the clutter, acquiring, and so forth, to how others who know you think about it. What have other people in your life told you about their perceptions of your hoarding problem? Have they told you that you have a lot of clutter, or just a little bit of clutter? Do they think that acquiring is a problem for you? Do you agree or disagree with what they say? Here's a self-assessment tool to help clarify how well your perceptions match up with those of other people.

●━ Comparing Your Perceptions With Those of Others

This questionnaire has 10 questions. The first 5 are for the person who has (or might have) a hoarding problem. The second 5 are for someone else to answer *about* the person who has (or might have) a hoarding problem. To complete this measure, then, you'll need to find a trusted person—a friend or family member, perhaps even a therapist or other social service worker. The important thing is to find someone who has actually seen your home and is in a good position to comment on the severity of the problem.

These first 5 questions are for the person who has (or might have) a hoarding problem.

1. Because of the clutter or number of possessions, how difficult is it for you to use the rooms in your home?

0	1	2	3	4	5	6	7	8
Not at all difficult		Mildly difficult		Moderately difficult		Severely difficult		Extremely difficult

2. To what extent do you have difficulty discarding (or recycling, selling, giving away) ordinary things that other people would get rid of?

0	1	2	3	4	5	6	7	8
No difficulty		Mild difficulty		Moderate difficulty		Severe difficulty		Extreme difficulty

3. To what extent do you currently have a problem with collecting free things or buying more things than you need or can use or can afford?

0	1	2	3	4	5	6	7	8
No problem		Mild problem		Moderate problem		Severe problem		Extreme problem

4. To what extent do you experience emotional distress because of clutter, difficulty discarding, or problems with buying or acquiring things?

0	1	2	3	4	5	6	7	8
None		Mild		Moderate		Severe		Extreme

5. To what extent do you experience impairment in your life (daily routine, job/school, social activities, family activities, financial difficulties) because of clutter, difficulty discarding, or problems with buying or acquiring things?

0	1	2	3	4	5	6	7	8
None		Mild		Moderate		Severe		Extreme

These next 5 questions are for *a friend, family member, or other trusted person.* Answer these questions about the person who has (or might have) a hoarding problem.

1. Because of the clutter or number of possessions, how difficult is it for this person to use the rooms in his/her home?

0	1	2	3	4	5	6	7	8
Not at all difficult		Mildly difficult		Moderately difficult		Severely difficult		Extremely difficult

2. To what extent does this person have difficulty discarding (or recycling, selling, giving away) ordinary things that other people would get rid of?

0	1	2	3	4	5	6	7	8
No difficulty		Mild difficulty		Moderate difficulty		Severe difficulty		Extreme difficulty

3. To what extent does this person currently have a problem with collecting free things or buying more things than he/she needs or can use or can afford?

0	1	2	3	4	5	6	7	8
No problem		Mild problem		Moderate problem		Severe problem		Extreme problem

4. To what extent does this person experience emotional distress because of clutter, difficulty discarding, or problems with buying or acquiring things?

0	1	2	3	4	5	6	7	8
None		Mild		Moderate		Severe		Extreme

5. To what extent does this person experience impairment in his/her life (daily routine, job/school, social activities, family activities, financial difficulties) because of clutter, difficulty discarding, or problems with buying or acquiring things?

0	1	2	3	4	5	6	7	8
None		Mild		Moderate		Severe		Extreme

Now, compare your answers. Did you and the other person generally agree about the severity of the problem, or were there significant areas of disagreement? If you disagreed by more than one point, this would be a great time to talk it over (but not argue!) with that person. Find out why he or she answered the questions the way he or she did. What might be some reasons for the disagreement?

One possible reason for disagreement is that your family member or friend does not recognize the important role your things play in your life. After all, the meaning of things is very personal and subjective, so you might see great value in something others don't. Your family or friends are likely making judgments based on how *they* would value your possessions, not on how *you* value them. So we'd like you to take a moment and ask yourself these tough questions:

- Do I view my possessions differently from how others view them?
- Do I overestimate the significance, value, or usefulness of objects?

Perhaps we're not the first to ask you these kinds of questions—in many cases, questions such as these get tossed about in arguments. But rather than going into argument mode, try being brutally honest with yourself. What do your answers to these questions tell you? Do they suggest that you need to change something?

Another possibility is that your family, friends, or other people are responding to how much the quantity of your stuff interferes with your ability to function. So here's another tough question for you to ask yourself:

- Can you honestly say that acquiring and saving things to the extent that you currently do has improved your life?

To answer this question, you need to take a step back and not think about how important your things are to you, but instead think about the things you don't or can't do because of your hoarding. Take a moment and go back to the Activities of Daily Living scale you completed in Chapter 3. Based on your answers, now ask yourself:

- How much of your life is restricted by your clutter or hoarding?
- How important is it to you to reclaim those parts of your life?

✳ Readiness to Work on the Problem

In Chapter 4, you completed a self-assessment exercise called "Are You Ready to Change?" Go back and take a peek at your answers. Do you still feel the same way, or, as often happens, has your level of readiness changed since then? Remember that readiness tends to wax and wane over time, and your level of readiness on one day may not be identical to your level of readiness the next.

✳ Telling Your Story

When making a major life change, it can be helpful to review what brought you to your current situation. Take a few minutes to outline how you got here. Answering a few questions might help you get started.

1. When did this problem begin?

2. When did it get out of control?

3. How have your family and friends reacted?

4. Are there major life events or trauma associated with this?

5. What things have you lost out on because of the clutter/hoarding?

6. What have you tried to control it? How did that work out?

Failure to understand or acknowledge the severity of clutter or acquiring is an all-too-common problem among people with hoarding problems and reflects what we call **limited insight** into the troublesome nature of the symptoms—in this case, clutter, difficulty getting rid of items, and perhaps also acquiring too many things. Even people who actually seek help for clutter become ambivalent when they are faced with difficult decisions about discarding or categorizing and putting away their things. Motivational techniques have been very helpful for other problems, like alcohol addiction, in which denial is common.

This requires a non-confrontational approach in which you try to step into the person's shoes to see it completely from his or her perspective. Then, ask questions and make comments that are genuinely motivated, not snide or condescending. For example, when the person has just denied that there is any problem, you can summarize calmly: "You don't really feel there is any problem. You are quite happy with the way the house looks." Remember, don't be sarcastic, just be clear and direct. This restatement of what the person has just said helps him or her feel heard and is less likely to make him or her feel defensive. More than likely, the person will respond with something like, "Well, I'm not completely happy. It is more stuff than I want, but I will get to it." This is a partial admission of a problem and moves just a little closer to being willing to work on it. Go on with, "You plan to get to it but haven't been able to yet. What do you think you need to get to it?" Again, say this calmly, with curiosity. This might move the person closer to talking about his or her struggle, again a further step in admitting a problem and considering working on it.

Of course, after the person's initial denial, you could have said, "But look at all that clutter! It's a fire hazard!" Imagine how you'd react to this if your situations were reversed. You'd dig in your heels, deny the danger or inconvenience, and defend the importance of your things and your right to keep them. So, this strategy really doesn't work to help motivate someone to work on the problem. But a direct statement that empathizes with the person's perspective reduces his or her defensiveness and often helps him or her to reconsider his or her position.

It is important to recognize that you probably feel conflicted about changing the way you acquire and save possessions. Many, perhaps most, people who hoard experience *ambivalence.* Ambivalence is not the same thing as apathy. Apathy means that one simply doesn't care at all about the problem. The fact that you're reading this book, and have made it this far, suggests to us that you are not apathetic. Ambivalence means *having opposing beliefs or feelings at the same time.* For example, you may feel desperate to get rid of the stacks of newspapers in your living room, but at the same time feel that you can't afford

Ambivalence is not the same thing as apathy.

to lose the information they contain. You want very much to have more space in your bedroom, but giving away any of your clothing, even things you no longer wear, seems impossible. There are two important things you must understand about ambivalence:

1. Ambivalence is natural and normal. Everyone experiences it, and it's especially likely to occur when people have conflicting needs, wants, or values. So there's nothing wrong with being ambivalent.

2. Now is the time to face ambivalence head on and work through it with the exercises contained in this book. It is very important that you explore both sides of this ambivalence, your wish to clear the clutter and your reluctance to part with your things.

We mentioned in Chapter 4 that people tend to work on a problem when the reasons for doing so clearly outweigh the reasons for not doing so. We call this the "balance of change." Understanding *your* balance of change is an important step. Figure 7.1 will probably look familiar; you saw something like it in Chapter 4. Now we'd like you to write on the figure your own reasons for working on the problem, as well as your reasons for not working on the problem. If you need help generating ideas, take a look at the sample in Chapter 4.

Which way does your balance of change seem to tip? If it tips toward change, most likely you are ready to begin working on the problem. On the other hand, if it tips toward not changing, this is a sign that working on hoarding may not be a particularly high priority for you: unless you find more reasons to change, there isn't much point even trying to clear the clutter. You'll just find excuses and have little success.

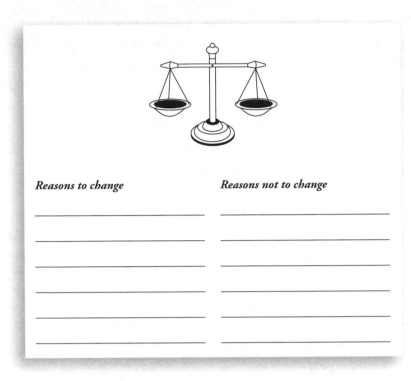

Reasons to change   *Reasons not to change*

_____   _____

_____   _____

_____   _____

_____   _____

_____   _____

_____   _____

Figure 7.1 Your Balance of Change Scale.

✳ Values and Personal Goals

Before going further, it may be helpful to answer a simple question. What do you value most in life? Is it family? Friendships? Work? Spirituality? List the four or five things most close to your heart.

My list of things I value most.

1.

2.

3.

4.

5.

Now, think about how your hoarding influences each of these values. Does the clutter and hoarding hurt your relationships with family and friends? Does it interfere with your work? Does it enhance any of the things you value? These are questions to think about as you work through this program and make decisions about what to keep and what to get rid of. You can also use them to establish concrete goals for the program. Think about what you want to accomplish, and how you want things to be when you're finished with the program. Think about what you would like your life to be like in 5 years. Like all

Think about what you want to accomplish, and how you want things to be when you're finished with the program.

the exercises in this book, this one will be most helpful if you get a pencil right now and write your answers down here, rather than just thinking about them.

We asked Helen (from Chapter 2) to list some of her goals and reasons for wanting to change. Here's what she came up with:

My personal goals for this program are:

1.   *I want to be safe in my house.*

2.   *I want to be able to find things I need.*

3.   *I want my home to be tidy enough to have people over without feeling embarrassed.*

4.   *I want to be able to cook in my kitchen again.*

I want to beat hoarding because:

1.   *My family is worried that I'll fall and hurt myself.*

2.   *I'm lonely and don't have enough company.*

3.   *I miss being able to enjoy my hobbies.*

4.   *I get frustrated with how chaotic everything is.*

If I work on my hoarding problem, the following things are likely to happen:

1. *I will be able to have my friends and family over to my house.*

2. *I will be able to cook again.*

3. *I will be able to find things more easily.*

If I don't work on my hoarding problem, the following things are likely to happen:

1. *I might fall and hurt myself.*

2. *I'll continue to be isolated and alone.*

3. *I'll continue to be unhappy.*

Bill had a harder time with this task. It was tough for him to come up with reasons to change. But we felt it was still important for him to try. After giving it a lot of thought, here's what he wrote:

My personal goals for this program are:

1. *I want Social Services to leave me alone.*

2. *I want to have a better relationship with my daughter.*

3. *I want to be financially stable.*

I want to beat hoarding because:

1. *I'm sick of all of the phone calls and letters from Social Services.*

2. *I don't like arguing with my daughter; I miss the close relationship we used to have.*

3. *I'm running out of money because I keep buying things.*

If I work on my hoarding problem, the following things are likely to happen:

1. *I will get Social Services off my back and will be able to live in peace.*

2. *I will be able to talk to my daughter without it turning into an argument about clutter, and maybe our relationship will get better.*

3. *I'll have more money for things I really want to do.*

If I don't work on my hoarding problem, the following things are likely to happen:

1. *I could be evicted from my home.*

2. *My relationship with my daughter will not get better.*

3. *I will eventually go broke.*

A word of caution here. It's important that your goals be realistic and manageable. For example, if your home is in terrible condition, it would probably be unrealistic to have a goal that your house will be so gorgeous that it will be featured in *Better Homes and Gardens* or something like that. When you set goals too high, it is very discouraging when you don't reach them. So start by setting attainable goals that are realistic for you. Remember, if you meet all your goals, you can always set new ones. Similarly, it's most helpful for these to be *your* goals, not someone else's goals for you. In the long run, you'll be motivated best to work toward what *you* want for yourself. Now, you try it.

My personal goals for this program are:

1. _____

2. _____

3. _____

4. _____

5. _____

6. _____

We'd also like you to think about why you selected these goals—that is, why they are important to you. Please write your answers to the following questions:

I want to beat hoarding because:

1. _____

2. _____

3. _____

4. _____

5. _____

If I work on my hoarding problem, the following things are likely to happen:

1. _____

2. _____

3. _____

4. _____

5. _____

If I don't work on my hoarding problem, the following things are likely to happen:

1. _____

2. _____

3. _____

4. _____

5. _____

It will be very important to remember these goals and consequences when the going gets rough. When you are having trouble deciding to get rid of clutter or not acquire something, look back at these goals and values. Decide whether the object in your hand is more important to you than your personal goals and values. Looking back at these will help you keep your long-term focus in the face of your short-term wishes.

 ## Motivation Boosters

Visualization Exercises

For these exercises, we'd like you to go to a part of your home that is currently cluttered. Bring this book with you, as well as a pencil or pen, and stand or sit somewhere that allows you to see most or all of the room. You might find it helpful to repeat the exercises in multiple areas of your home.

━◠ Clutter Visualization Exercise

A. Look around the room, noticing the clutter. Turn slowly so you can see all of it.

B. How uncomfortable did you feel while looking around this room? Circle a number on the scale below:

    0   1   2   3   4   5   6   7   8   9   10
    no discomfort   severe discomfort

C. What feelings were you having while looking around this room?

    1. _____

    2. _____

    3. _____

D. What thoughts or beliefs were you having while looking around this room?

    1. _____

    2. _____

    3. _____

A. Now visualize this room with the clutter gone (it might help to close your eyes when you do this). Imagine cleared surfaces and floors, tabletops without piles, and uncluttered floors with only rugs and furniture. For now, don't worry about where the things have gone; just imagine the room without clutter.

B. How uncomfortable did you feel while imagining this room uncluttered? Circle a number on the scale below:

0   1   2   3   4   5   6   7   8   9   10

no discomfort   severe discomfort

C. What thoughts and feelings were you having while visualizing this room?

1. _____

2. _____

3. _____

D. Imagine what you can do in this room now that it is not cluttered. Picture how pleasant this room will feel when you have arranged it the way you want it. Describe your thoughts and feelings.

1. _____

2. _____

3. _____

E. How uncomfortable did you feel while imagining the room this way? Use the scale below:

0   1   2   3   4   5   6   7   8   9   10

no discomfort   severe discomfort

✳ A Contract With Yourself

People tend to stick with a plan best when they make a clear, formal declaration of intent. That's why we recommend you sign an agreement with the one person you are most responsible and accountable to—yourself. If you can give a copy to another person you trust, it might be even more effective.

> *People tend to stick with a plan best when they make a clear, formal declaration of intent.*

➤ Treatment Contract

I, _____, make this promise to myself:

- I will work on my hoarding problem to the best of my ability.
- I will make beating hoarding a priority in my life, and I will work hard not to let other things distract me from this goal.
- I will work on the problem actively for at least _____ minutes/hours per day, _____ days per week.
- I will praise and reward myself when I work hard on hoarding.
- I will not beat myself up when I make mistakes, but I will renew my efforts.
- Other promise(s) you would like to make to yourself:

Signature _____ Date _____

Coming Back to This Chapter

Of course, after the person's initial denial, you could have said, "But look at all that clutter! It's a fire hazard!" Imagine how you'd react to this if your situations were reversed. You'd dig in your heels, deny the danger or inconvenience, and defend the importance of your things and your right to keep them. So, this strategy really doesn't work to help motivate someone to work on the problem. But a direct statement that empathizes with the person's perspective reduces his or her defensiveness and often helps him or her to reconsider his or her position.

Fact File for Family and Friends

Helping Others with Motivation

It's hard to know what to do when your loved one seems less motivated than you are to work on the problem. Often, it's tempting to start arguing with the person, trying to persuade him or her to see things the way you do: "Why can't you see it my way, just for a minute?" "One of these days, they're going to find your dead body under a pile of trash!" "Can't you see what this is doing to your family?"

The problem is that this kind of direct confrontation rarely works. Perhaps you have already noticed this, that the harder you argue, the more your loved one argues back, makes excuses, ignores you, or avoids working on the clutter. So you try arguing even harder, being even more persuasive. And then your loved one argues back even harder, ignores you even more, and so on. If this pattern sounds familiar to you, the confrontational approach simply is not working and it's time to try something else.

In our work with lots of people who hoard, you might be surprised to learn that we almost never tell them what to do. We don't tell them to throw things away, nor do we tell them not to acquire things. Why? Because it doesn't work. Instead, we find that the best way to help people increase their motivation to work on the problem is to use principles developed by Drs. William Miller and Steven Rollnick for helping people make decisions about major behavioral changes.

There are three key assumptions we'd like you to keep in mind:

1. *Ambivalence is normal.* It's very rare for someone to want anything 100 percent, with no hesitation. Especially when people are trying to decide whether or not to make a dramatic lifestyle change, it is perfectly normal for them to have mixed feelings and thoughts. Part of them wants to change,

and part of them doesn't want to change. The person feels conflicted and seems to "flip-flop" from one moment to the next. The important thing is to remember that this is normal and healthy.

2. *People have a right to make their own choices.* There are, of course, some exceptions to this, such as minors or adults who have been found legally not competent to look after their own affairs, and who have a legally appointed guardian. For the most part, however, we should and must respect people's freedom of choice.

3. *Nothing will happen until the person is ready to change.* You can't rush it. If the person's "balance of change" (see earlier in this chapter) is still tipped toward not changing, he or she is not going to sustain the level of effort and interest that it takes to change. The key, therefore, is to help the person understand and weigh all the factors so he or she can make an informed choice. You can't argue him or her into it.

"OK," you might be thinking, "I understand that the confrontational approach won't work, and that nothing's going to change until the person is ready. But how can I help my loved one get ready? It's not going to happen spontaneously!" We agree: people with longstanding behavior problems such as hoarding rarely just decide to change out of the blue. So you should definitely talk about the problem with your loved one, just in a different way.

We should note here that the conversational pointers we list here will only be helpful within the context of a trusting and supportive relationship. Sometimes, that's not the case. For

(continued)

example, we've seen many relationships that have been terribly damaged by hoarding or other issues. If you and your loved one don't already have a common bond of trust and support—if every conversation seems to end up with yelling, name-calling, or door-slamming—you're likely to have difficulty changing gears. Consider having someone else be the designated support person, or consider getting outside help for a damaged relationship if that seems necessary.

Here are some general principles to guide your conversations.

Show Empathy

Showing empathy doesn't necessarily mean that you agree with everything the person says, but it does mean you are willing to listen and to try to see things from the other person's perspective. Empathy must come from the heart—be sure you are not being patronizing. A good rule is that if you don't truly mean what you're about to say, don't say it. Here are some good ways to show empathy:

- Ask open-ended questions—that is, questions that can't be answered with a simple "yes" or "no." It might be particularly useful to ask some questions that will help you understand what your loved one finds rewarding about the possessions: "What are some things you like about these items?" "What does it feel like when you pick something up?" "How are you feeling right now?"
- Summarize your understanding of what your loved one says: "I think I hear you saying that right now cleaning up the clutter is not a high priority for you; do I have that right?"
- Make statements about what your loved one seems to be feeling, so he or she knows you're paying attention: "It looks

like you're feeling anxious right now." "Your voice sounds kind of sad; do you want to talk about that?"
- Use compliments and statements of appreciation and understanding: "You're really being brave right now." "I know how hard this is, and I appreciate the fact you're willing to work on it."

Don't Argue

Ever. There is simply no point in arguing about hoarding. The harder you argue, the more the person is likely to argue back. This is more than just a waste of time: it's a well-known fact that the more we say something, the more we tend to believe it. So when you engage your loved one in an argument about hoarding, you are essentially putting him or her in a position to make the argument for NOT changing, again and again and again. And the more he or she makes that argument, the more believable it will seem. The solution is to get out of the argument. Watch out for:

- Ordering, directing, or commanding
- Warning or threatening
- Persuading with logic, arguing, or lecturing
- Moralizing, preaching, or telling your loved one what he or she "should" do
- Judging, criticizing, or blaming

Respect Autonomy

Remember, most of you are dealing with an adult who has freedom of choice about his or her own possessions. You do not have to like the condition of his or her home, nor do you have to be happy about his or her behavior. If the person with the hoarding problem is your spouse and lives with you, or if the hoarding behavior infringes on your personal living space, you do have a right to ask the person to change. But

(continued)

even in these circumstances, you will be most effective when you reassure your loved one that you are not trying to take away his or her autonomy. Try to engage your loved one in a discussion (rather than an argument) about the home and his or her behavior. Talk about your concerns in an open and frank manner, without being confrontational, argumentative, or hostile. Ask your loved one what he or she wants to do, rather than just telling him or her what you want: "What do you think *you* would like to do about the clutter in the home?" "How do *you* suggest we proceed?"

Perhaps at this point you're thinking, "Now wait a minute. My loved one has a serious hoarding problem, and it's really important that he or she does something about it. So instead of telling them how terrible the problem is, I'm just supposed to be empathic, stop arguing, and ask what he or she wants to do? How will anything change that way?" We have two answers. First, before anything can get better, it is imperative that you put the brakes on things that are not working. Remember that old joke: The definition of insanity is doing the same thing over and over, expecting a different result! You might be surprised by how much more smoothly things seem to go when you just focus on stopping unproductive, confrontational discussions. Second, we have one more principle to tell you, which will help your loved one think about changing from a perspective that will be more meaningful to him or her: *Help the person recognize that his or her actions are inconsistent with his or her greater goals or values.* Some ways to facilitate this recognition include:

- Ask the person about his or her goals and values. Recognize that those goals and values might not be the same as yours. "What's really important to you in life?"

"How would you like your life to be 5 years from now?" "What are your hopes and goals in life?"

- Discuss whether or not the person's acquiring or difficulty organizing or getting rid of things fits with those goals and values. This is most effective if you ask, rather than tell. "How does the condition of your home fit with your desire to be a good grandmother?" "You've told me that friendships are very important to you; how well can you pursue that goal, given the way things are right now?"

If you have been accustomed to arguing and threatening and blaming, your new approaches will surprise your loved one, and it may take a little time before the person begins to trust you. Try these methods in several conversations and notice whether the balance seems to be tilting in the right direction. If so, be patient and keep up the good work. Please keep in mind that your interaction patterns with family members are longstanding habits that may be hard to break. Be gentle with yourself as you try to change the way you interact.

Set Limits

If your best efforts do not help the person see how his or her personal goals and hoarding behavior don't match, you may need to set personal limits to cope with your own needs. Be very careful to do this calmly and without arguing. Decide what you can and cannot tolerate with regard to your own personal needs and space or those of others (children, elderly people) you are responsible for. Tell your family member (1) how you feel, (2) what you want, and (3) what you will do. State your feelings and your request

(continued)

clearly: "Susan, those piles you left on my desk make me very upset. That is my space and you do not have the right to put things there. Please remove the pile by the end of this week." Or you might say, "Billy needs a place to sleep that is his own. The stuff you put on his bed has to be gone by Thursday." Then state what you will do or not do: "If you can't do this yourself, I'll put it into a box and take it to the basement." Don't be punitive; just remove the clutter after fair warning. You can give a simple reminder, but remember to avoid using an unpleasant tone. If the request is not met by the deadline, you should carry out the stated consequence. Your loved one is likely to be upset with you, so remember to stay calm, "I told you I would move those things by Thursday. I understand that this upsets you and I am sorry about that. I tried to be as clear as I could about what I needed and what would happen."

Obviously, it is not ideal to move things that belong to someone else when this upsets them. However, we all have our personal limits that we must protect. If stating your own feelings and setting limits helps your family member keep his or her things out of your space, you have accomplished your goal. If this does not work and your loved one's hoarding behavior continues to be seriously problematic in your relationship, you will want to seek help for your relationship.

8

Reducing Acquiring

✳ Motivation Booster

Take a few moments to think about how you acquire things. For most
people with hoarding problems, excessive acquisition is a problem, and they
recognize it. Sometimes, however, it isn't always clear to people that their
acquiring (buying or collecting free things) is out of control. It can be a fun
activity, especially when other aspects of life are not so fun. As you get farther along in this program, it will become clear to you whether or not your
acquisition is a problem. By now, you may have a good idea whether you
have a significant problem acquiring too many things—buying too much
or finding free things. You may or may not have listed reducing acquiring
as one of your goals in Chapter 7. Take a moment to think about your goals
for controlling your acquiring. At the end of this chapter, we've provided
you with a note card that you can cut out (or, if you prefer, you can make
a copy of it). Write your goals for controlling acquiring and why you want
to achieve them on the card, and put it in your purse or wallet next to your
money or credit cards. Get into the habit of looking at it each time you get
set to buy something. If acquiring free things is the problem, tape the note
card to the dashboard of your car.

As you learned in Chapter 6, you may have trouble because you really
enjoy getting new stuff; it's like an addiction that's hard to control. Maybe
you do it because you're in a bad mood and going to flea markets makes you
feel better. Maybe you start out needing something and when you get to the
store, you see lots of stuff that seems like a good buy, even if you don't really
need it. Whatever the reason, the methods in this chapter will help you get

your acquiring under control. This will take practice in many different situations where you've acquired things in the past.

✳ The Avoidance Solution

If you are hooked on Saturday morning yard sales, find something else to do.

Many people who can't control their acquiring end up avoiding the places where they have problems. To begin gaining control over your acquiring, this is a good place to start. If you are hooked on Saturday morning yard sales, find something else to do. Unfortunately, avoidance is not a very good long-term solution. Our lives are filled with signals to buy or acquire. Eventually you will find yourself in a situation where your urge to acquire will be very strong. You need something that gives you control over your urges and will allow you to go into any situation without fear of losing that control. This chapter will help you develop that control.

✳ The Control Solution

The hardest part of solving your acquiring problem is resisting strong urges. This is a struggle between the short-term payoff—feeling good right now—versus the long-term cost—making your hoarding problem worse. In this chapter you will learn ways to develop control over your urges to acquire and to remove emotion from the process of acquiring. This will be a four-step process:

1. You will figure out how and why you have trouble with acquiring.

2. You will develop strategies to think differently about your acquiring decisions.

3. You will use these strategies in a series of "non-shopping" trips so that you can learn how to better tolerate your triggers and urges to acquire.

4. You will develop strategies for finding enjoyment and coping in other ways.

Step 1: Discovering What, How, and Why You Acquire

The first step in the process of reducing acquiring is to know how and why you acquire. To truly know this, we'd like you to track your acquiring for a week or two, recording everything that comes into the house. We mean everything—delivery packages, store purchases (plus the bags and receipts), handouts and flyers you picked up, newspapers and magazines, demo freebies, gifts from others, subscriptions to magazines and newspapers, catalog orders, TV purchases, Internet buys, things picked out of the trash, stuff from yard sales or flea markets, extras purchased "just in case," even (for some people) stolen items. Keep a record of anything that crosses the threshold of your home. The form below will help you do this. It also has a place to put how uncomfortable you would feel if you didn't get the item. This gives you an idea of which items will be hardest to resist, and it will be useful when you develop a list for practicing not acquiring.

Track your acquiring for a week or two, recording everything that comes into the house.

☞ My Acquiring Form

List everything you got and how you got it.

How uncomfortable would you feel if you didn't get it?
0 = fine 10 = awful

_____   _____

_____   _____

_____   _____

_____   _____

_____   _____

_____   _____

_____   _____

_____   _____

_____   _____

_____   _____

✳ Understanding Your Acquiring: The Compulsive Acquiring Process

Usually a buying or acquiring episode begins with an EMOTIONAL VULNERABILITY. Recall Bill from Chapter 2, who anticipated his trips to flea markets with great delight. Helen's episodes, on the other hand, were usually preceded by anxiety and feeling overwhelmed. Different people may acquire in reaction to different emotional states.

While in this emotional state, a TRIGGER or cue for acquiring usually sets off the episode. For Bill it was the sight of a potential treasure. For Helen it was notice of a sale on clothes. The trigger is the thing you see, hear, or otherwise experience that gets you really thinking about acquiring.

THOUGHTS about oneself and acquiring determine what happens next. For Bill, the thoughts were of how wonderful it would be to acquire a treasure. He had an elaborate and extensive set of thoughts about the usefulness and value of the treasure, but virtually no thoughts about the costs or disadvantages of buying. For Helen, the thoughts were about how this thing might make her feel better and, quite emphatically, that she deserved to feel better. As with Bill, she had few thoughts about the costs or disadvantages of buying. The deck was stacked for both Bill and Helen.

Once you have acquired the item, you experience an IMMEDIATE EMOTIONAL PAYOFF. For Bill and Helen, acquiring their treasures led to an immediate feeling of relief and joy, and even a sense of victory. As you know by now, whenever there's a payoff for doing something, you're more likely to do it again and again. It's the payoff that "hooks" you.

Of course, the immediate emotional payoff doesn't last forever. After the "high" of acquiring wears off (this could be anywhere from a few minutes to a few weeks after the acquisition), REGRET kicks in. Bill and Helen both eventually realized that they had spent money they needed for other things and that they didn't have room for their treasures. The realization that their new purchases went onto the piles and contributed to their already cluttered homes was depressing.

Before long, the regret often turns to some pretty serious NEGATIVE CONCLUSIONS about yourself. After a while, Bill thought to himself,

"I am weak." Helen thought, "There is something wrong with me" and even, "I am worthless." These kinds of thoughts tend to deepen negative moods like sadness and frustration. How did Bill and Helen cope with their unhappy moods? By acquiring more! And on it goes.

To break this vicious cycle, you must understand how each part of this process works for you: beginning emotional state, acquiring trigger, thoughts that lead to acquiring, immediate emotional consequences, regret, and negative conclusions about oneself.

A good way to start is to picture one or two recent situations when this happened. Pick something from the acquiring form that you can remember pretty well. Now think back to the minutes and hours before, during, and after you got it. Fill in the details for each of the six steps in the process. Try to provide the most detail for the first three steps.

1. Beginning emotional state:
    a. _____
    b. _____
    c. _____

2. Acquiring trigger(s):
    a. _____
    b. _____
    c. _____

3. Thoughts that make acquiring more likely:
    a. _____
    b. _____
    c. _____
    d. _____
    e. _____

4. Immediate emotional experience after acquiring:
    a. _____
    b. _____
    c. _____

5. Development of regret:
    a. _____
    b. _____

6. Negative conclusions about yourself:

   a. _____

   b. _____

To gain control over your acquiring, you must find a way to change your responses to the first three steps of the compulsive acquiring process. We will cover these in reverse order, beginning with "thoughts that make acquiring more likely."

✳ Step 2: Changing Your Thoughts About Acquiring

Many people who acquire compulsively seem to lose themselves in the moment—that is, they get "hyper-focused," forgetting about the rest of their lives and thinking only about the item in front of them. Much of what you will learn here involves keeping the rest of your life in focus as you make decisions about acquiring.

Setting Rules and Asking Questions

The simplest and most straightforward way to think differently while shopping or acquiring is to establish a firm set of rules to go by. Here are some rules that might work for you:

I cannot get this unless:

- I plan to use it within the next month.
- I have enough money right now to pay for it.
- I have a place to put it so it doesn't add to the clutter.
- I am sure I truly want this and will not return it.
- Acquiring this item is consistent with my goals and values for my life.
- I have a true NEED, not just a wish, for this item.

Some rules might be temporary. For example, you might want to stop buying any new magazines until you have read a certain number of those you already have. We've included these rules on the card at the end of this chapter.

Another good strategy to change your thinking during acquisition is to generate a set of questions to challenge your thinking. Carrying these with you and asking them before acquiring can help keep your life in focus and your decisions more in line with your goals.

Here are some examples:

- Do I already own something similar?
- Am I buying this because I feel bad (angry, depressed, etc.) right now?
- Will I regret getting this in a week?
- Could I manage without it?
- Do I have enough time to fix/use this, or do I have more important priorities?
- Do I want it just because I'm looking at it now?
- Will *not* getting this help me solve my hoarding problem?

Based on what you've learned here, fill in the Non-Acquiring Help Card (following page 120) and carry it with you. Consult it whenever you are thinking of acquiring something. See if it changes your acquiring patterns.

Think Through the Advantages and Disadvantages

Another method for dealing with these thoughts is to take a few minutes to think about the advantages of buying something new versus the disadvantages of doing so. You can do this in two lists to help you see how these stack up against each other. For example, Helen had urges to buy more clothes, so we asked her to come up with some advantages and disadvantages of buying more clothes. Here's what she wrote:

Advantages of buying more clothes
- *Feeling good about having new things to wear*
- *Reducing bad feelings if I'm in a funk*
- *Not losing out on a good bargain*

Disadvantages of buying more clothes
- *Spending more money than I should*
- *Feeling guilty*

- *Making it harder to go on the vacation I really want*
- *Adding to the clutter in my bedroom*
- *Making my husband mad because I spent money I shouldn't have*

Not only were there more disadvantages than advantages, but you might notice as well that the disadvantages also seem stronger, more compelling. Helen could also have thought about the advantages of NOT buying more clothes, especially the emotional advantages. For example, she would probably feel more in control, better able to choose, instead of feeling compelled to buy.

Now you try it. Think of an item that you would like to acquire, and write down your advantages and disadvantages on the worksheet provided.

●← Advantages/Disadvantages Worksheet

What's the item? _____

_____

Advantages (Benefits) of acquiring: Disadvantages (Costs) of acquiring:

Step 3: Learning to Tolerate Your Triggers to Acquire

Triggers to acquire can be anything. For one of our clients, a particular exit from the highway (that led to the mall) was one of her triggers to go shopping. Triggers can unleash powerful urges to acquire that may seem impossible to control. It is no surprise that people learn to avoid triggers in order to prevent these overpowering urges. As we noted, however, avoidance is ineffective or only partially effective as a long-term solution. What we outline here is a strategy for learning how to tolerate these urges. Once you learn to tolerate them, they will become less intense and have less power over you.

The way you will do this is by exposing yourself to gradually more powerful acquiring triggers. As you are able to tolerate minimal urges provoked by "weak" triggers, using the thinking strategies discussed earlier, you will then be able to expose yourself to more intense triggers and more powerful urges, going slowly enough that you are able to tolerate the increasing intensity.

Creating a Non-Acquiring Hierarchy

To begin, make a list of all the acquiring triggers you can think of. Once you have a list, rate how intense your acquiring urges are for each of these triggers. You can also think of this as how much discomfort you would feel if you ignored the trigger and did not acquire. From your list of acquiring triggers, start with those that would bother you only slightly, perhaps 1 or 2 on the urge/discomfort scale, and then put down those that you would rate 3 or 4. Work your way on up, making sure that all of the situations in which you commonly acquire are listed.

We asked Bill to think of several triggers to acquire and then to rank them from least to most discomfort:

✳ Bill's Non-Acquiring Hierarchy

Situation	Urge/Discomfort (0–10)
1. *Driving past things others have left on the curb*	1
2. *Driving past a yard sale*	2
3. *Driving past the dollar store*	2
4. *Walking past a yard sale in my neighborhood*	3
5. *Walking into the dollar store and looking around*	4
6. *Walking around the tables at a yard sale*	5
7. *Walking around at a yard sale without buying*	6
8. *Picking things up at a yard sale without buying*	7
9. *Picking things up at a dollar store without buying*	8
10. *Picking up a "treasure" that someone has left on the curb*	9

From Planning to Practice

Now it is time to put your planning into practice. This means exposing yourself gradually to the situations from your list. Pick the first item from your list and think about whether you are prepared to work on this. Your task in all of this practice is to tolerate the urge and discomfort until the tasks get easier and easier. This will take some time and some repeated practice, but it will get easier. We usually recommend gradual steps, beginning with drive-by non-shopping excursions, then walking through a store without touching, and finally the hardest step, handling things without buying or otherwise acquiring them.

If you are very fearful, one way to reduce discomfort is by visualizing the situation before you actually go there. Close your eyes and imagine being in the situation. Notice how you feel and what you are thinking. Now imagine leaving the situation without the item you want. How much discomfort (0–10) did you experience while imagining? Now think about why you might NOT want to acquire this item. What are the disadvantages of getting it? Focusing hard on these will probably help reduce how upset you feel. If you are still somewhat uncomfortable or worried you might not be able to resist, you might want to repeat this imagining before you actually do the experiment.

Also consider whether you want someone to go with you. The person should be someone who can help you resist the urge to buy or acquire, not encourage you to do so. These practice sessions can be harder than you think. The pleasure from acquiring can be very compelling!

When you practice not acquiring, it takes time for your level of discomfort to go down. Therefore, we recommend you keep a record of your discomfort (using the 0–10 scale) about every 10 minutes, or whenever you notice a change. How long you should stay depends on how quickly your discomfort decreases. Your goal is to leave feeling better than when you started the non-acquiring task. Ideally, you would feel that your urge to acquire was under your own control, even if you still wanted the items you saw. The first few times you practice will be hardest because you are fighting longstanding habits. Gradually, you will feel more in control. As you practice not acquiring or buying and see that nothing bad happens, your urges to acquire will become weaker. Notice whether you used any other special coping methods that seemed to work well for you, because you'll want to remember these in case of future need.

Step 4: Developing Alternative Sources of Enjoyment and Coping

Another critical component is to find other activities that replace the enjoyment that acquiring provides. What would you like to do instead of going to flea markets or yard sales on Saturday? Brainstorm a short list of choices, especially ones you can do at a moment's notice, either by yourself or with others. You should come up with a mixture of things you can do at home and outside the home. Here are some suggestions, but remember that your own ideas will work best:

- Visit a museum or other place of interest (historic home, local fair).
- Go to a library and check out books you'd like to read.
- Read a book.

- Watch a film in the theater or at home.
- Go to a restaurant with friends.
- Take a walk or hike with friends.
- Attend a talk or lecture.

Fact File for Family and Friends

Instructions for Coaches

One very helpful activity for coaches is to accompany the person on a non-acquiring trip. This means that you and the person will actually go to a location where the person likes to acquire things, such as a retail store, discount store, flea market, yard sale, etc. Here are some ways to make your involvement most helpful.

Help the person to remain focused on the task in front of him or her. As we've mentioned before, it's easy for people with hoarding problems to get "off task." The coach can be very helpful by politely reminding the person what he or she is supposed to be doing right now.

Provide emotional support. Rather than expressing anger or frustration at the person, express empathy with statements such as, "I can see how hard this is for you," or "I understand that you have mixed feelings about whether to buy this."

Help the person make decisions, but DO NOT make decisions for him or her. Encourage the person to think out loud about the possessions. Just listen and encourage him or her to consider questions that might help. These include:

- Do you really need this?
- Do you already have enough of these?
- Will this add something new?
- Do you have a specific plan to use this item?
- Will you really use it within a reasonable timeframe?
- What are the advantages of passing this up?
- What are the disadvantages of acquiring it?
- Is getting this good or bad for you?

- Do you have enough space for this?
- Do you want it taking up space in your home?
- Is this how you want to use the space you have?
- Will not getting this help you solve your hoarding problem?

Be a cheerleader. Congratulate the person for being brave, and tell him or her you know he or she can do it.

We have also found that even the most well-meaning coaches can make themselves less helpful by using the wrong strategies. Here are some DON'Ts:

Don't argue with the person about what to acquire. Long debates about the usefulness of an item or the need to get rid of it will only produce negative emotional reactions that don't facilitate progress. Instead, whenever you feel in conflict, take a break, relax a bit, and remind yourself how difficult this is for the person with the hoarding problem.

Don't take over decisions. Be sure the person with the hoarding problem is in charge at all times and makes all decisions, with the coach's support and guidance.

Don't work beyond your own tolerance level. To be a good coach, you have to take care of yourself first and then help your friend or family member. So feel free to set limits on how long and how much work you can do on any given occasion. Pat yourself on the back for your own efforts; helping someone who hoards is very hard work.

- Take an adult education class at the local high school.
- Attend a community meeting or gathering of interest.
- Work on a craft project you've been putting off.

We recommend putting the most interesting ideas at the top of the list and then posting them on your refrigerator, your calendar, or someplace else that will catch your attention. The list will be a reminder when your urge to acquire pops up. To get into new habits, you might want to assign yourself to actually do some of these things for practice in the next few weeks. When you do them, notice how much enjoyment you actually felt when you did it. You can use a simple scale, from 0 = no enjoyment to 10 = strong enjoyment. We predict you'll find that the other choices you made were more satisfying or fun than you had thought.

If you shop or collect to improve your mood, you will also need to find some other ways to cope with bad feelings like depression, guilt, or anger. Some of the activities you listed will probably help a lot. You might also want to find other coping strategies by using the problem-solving methods you learned in Chapter 5. For example, calling a friend or watching a funny program on TV may help to lighten your mood without encouraging any unwanted acquiring.

Non-Acquiring Help Card

My goals for reducing acquiring are:

1. _____

2. _____

3. _____

I want to achieve these goals because:

1. _____

2. _____

3. _____

I cannot get this unless:
- I plan to use it within the next month.
- I have enough money right now to pay for it.
- I have a place to put it so it doesn't add to the clutter.
- I am sure I truly want this and will not return it.
- Acquiring this item is consistent with my goals and values for my life.
- I have a true NEED, not just a wish, for this item.

Questions to ask yourself:
- Do I already own something similar?
- Am I buying this because I feel bad (angry, depressed, etc.) right now?
- Will I regret getting this in a week?
- Could I manage without it?
- Do I have enough time to fix/use this, or do I have more important priorities?
- Do I want it just because I'm looking at it now?
- Will *not* getting this help me solve my hoarding problem?
- _____
- _____
- _____

Figure 8.1

Sorting/Removing Stuff
Getting Ready

✳ Motivation Booster

OK, you're just about ready to start the major tasks in beating hoarding: sorting, organizing, and removing stuff. By now, we hope, you feel very ready to start the process. As you get started here, remember that you must develop your Practice Muscle. Your goal should be to work your Practice Muscle up to between 30 and 60 minutes each day. If at first you can work for only 5 minutes each day, do that for a few days and then move up to 10 minutes. The following week increase to 15 or 20 minutes and keep moving up until you reach 30 minutes. Keep on going up to 60 minutes if you possibly can, although it might not be all at once. Then you will start to see real progress.

✳ Work With Your Brain, Not Against It

Recall from Chapter 6 that people who hoard often experience difficulty sustaining attention (remember the buffalo?), solving problems, making decisions, and categorizing things. If this is true of you, we'll need to find a way to work around it. Even if it's not true of you, and it seems like your brain is working just fine, you will probably still find the ideas in this section helpful.

Often, people who hoard push their brains to the max, overloading them and making it even harder to accomplish the things they want to do.

Sometimes, what seems helpful in the short run might actually be harmful in the long run. For example, most people with hoarding problems use ineffective organizing strategies for their possessions. Helen, for example, was worried that she would forget something such as a bill that needed to be paid. To reduce this fear, she tried to keep all her mail in plain view, rather than putting it in a drawer, a file cabinet, or somewhere else where she couldn't see it. The problem with this strategy was that because Helen rarely threw any mail away, it piled up on her countertops, table, and other horizontal surfaces, to the point where she couldn't find anything, even if she wanted to. Helen was trying to compensate for what she thought were memory problems, but in the long run she actually made it *harder,* not easier, for her brain to keep track of things.

Bill wanted to organize his possessions, too, but he ran into trouble when he tried to sort things into categories. Because he felt many of his possessions were unique and special, he thought they needed to be in categories of their own. The end result was that he had lots and lots of very small categories and couldn't figure out what to do next. Bill had chosen an organizational strategy that felt right to him but ultimately couldn't work, even in the best of circumstances. When Bill started sorting, he found that his attention kept wandering to different topics. He knew he had a lot of work to do to get his possessions organized, but he couldn't stop his brain from thinking about other things. He started thinking about all the errands he had to run, bills he needed to pay, and so on. Sometimes, noises like the TV or his neighbors working outside distracted him as well. To keep himself on task, Bill had to train himself to *delay his distractibility.* Here's what he did:

1. He went to his local kitchen supply store and bought a kitchen timer that could be set to sound an alarm after a certain number of minutes.

2. First, he set the timer for 10 minutes, because that seemed to be about as long as he could concentrate.

3. He got rid of as many distractions as he could during his sorting and organizing sections. He turned off the TV and radio and even took his

phone off the hook. He put a sheet over the stuff that was out of reach so he couldn't see things he wasn't working on right then.

4. He practiced focusing on sorting and organizing for just 10 minutes at a time. When the timer alarm went off, he stopped and allowed himself to do other things for a while. He repeated this process three times a day until it felt relatively easy for him to maintain attention for 10 minutes.

5. Then, Bill tried setting the alarm for 15 minutes. He found it difficult at first, and his mind initially tended to wander after 10. However, he stuck with it, three times a day, and after a few days he was able to focus for 15 minutes without difficulty, then he increased it to 20 minutes and eventually 30 minutes. He began to see real progress in clearing spaces.

6. Next, Bill worked on strengthening his attention even more, using the timer. He worked until he started to feel bored or distracted, *then* he set the timer for 5 more minutes, and eventually 10 more. Now he was training himself to work past the point of distraction. When another idea came to his mind—for example, errands he had to run or other projects he wanted to work on—he quickly wrote it down on a piece of paper, telling himself, "I'll get to that later on." By writing it down, he knew he wouldn't forget it and could more stay focused on his top priority, working on his hoarding problem. Over several days, Bill found that he could work longer and longer past the point of distraction, until he was able to work on sorting and discarding for longer periods of time.

Bill also found it helpful to use a calendar to help him keep track of the things he needed to do. Previously, he had been trying to keep everything in his head, remembering what had to be done from day to day and week to week. Even though Bill's memory was pretty good, he found that keeping all of these things in his memory was overtaxing his mental resources and making it hard to stay focused. By writing down the things that he had to do, and updating his list frequently, Bill found that he did not have to memorize all of his plans and could therefore devote more attention to the task at hand.

We've provided some blank calendar pages in this chapter (Figure 9.1) for you to copy and use to keep track of the things you need to do. You may also download additional copies from the Treatments *That Work*™ Web site at www.oup.com/us/ttw. Alternatively, you might prefer to go to a store and buy a pocket or wall calendar for this purpose. If you prefer to use a computer or smart phone to keep track of your activities, as the authors of this book do, that's fine too. The important thing is to find a system you will actually use that makes things easier, not harder.

Another important step for Bill involved figuring out when his brain was at its best. Through some trial and error, Bill discovered that he was much sharper in the morning than in the afternoon or evening. As the day wore on, Bill noted that he became more tired, and it was harder for him to sustain attention. Because of this, Bill made a point of scheduling his sorting and organizing sessions for the morning. Think about how your brain works. When do you feel clearest and most capable of sustaining attention? When does your brain feels overburdened and less capable? Try scheduling your sorting and organizing sessions during the times your brain is most likely to cooperate.

People who hoard sometimes let fears of making mistakes get in their way. Helen told us, "What would happen if I accidentally threw away a bill that I was supposed to pay? The results could be devastating!" Because Helen was so afraid to make a mistake, she found the process of decision-making so unpleasant and burdensome that she often ended up delaying her decisions until the last minute. But would it have been so terrible if a bill went unpaid? Helen had the opportunity to find out for herself when, because she'd been avoiding decision-making, she forgot to pay a bill on time. She had half-expected the world to come crashing in on her, or perhaps the police to come breaking down her door for not paying the bill. In fact, the only consequence was that the company sent a second bill—hardly a consequence at all. It was not the end of the world, and Helen could see that her fears had been exaggerated.

Helen also found herself becoming easily overwhelmed by the sheer magnitude of the task: "There is so much to do; I hardly know where to start!"

Week of _____						
Monday ___	Tuesday ___	Wednesday ___	Thursday ___	Friday ___	Saturday ___	Sunday ___

Figure 9.1 Calendar

Whenever she would start to work on a particular area of her kitchen, she inevitably found her eyes going to other parts of the room, and she would tell herself how much there was still to do and how awful the task was going to be. As you can guess, this was not helping her. Helen found it helpful to take these steps to reduce the overwhelmed feeling:

1. She broke the big task down into several smaller tasks. Instead of working on her entire kitchen, for example, she selected one small area of her kitchen counter to work on. When she found her mind wandering to other parts of the kitchen, she gently reminded herself to stick with the smaller task in front of her. "I'll get to those other areas in due time," she said to herself.

2. She positioned herself so that her back was to the rest of the room. That way, she was able to minimize the amount of time she spent looking at parts of the room she was not working on.

Sorting and organizing can also be complicated by the presence of co-occurring conditions such as attention-deficit/hyperactivity disorder (ADHD) or obsessive-compulsive disorder (OCD). Both of these conditions seem to occur frequently in people who hoard, and they can make it quite difficult to stay focused on a task and make decisions in a timely manner. If you have one of these problems, or any other condition that affects your ability to pay attention and make decisions, it may be helpful for you to go very slowly through this part of the program. Take it one step at a time, and try to work on small "chunks" of the problem instead of the whole thing all at once. You might find it helpful to seek treatment from someone who specializes in these conditions, and/or take a look at the self-help manuals we mentioned in Chapter 1.

Develop a Systematic Strategy for Solving Problems

As you go through this process, it is to be expected that problems will arise. Things won't go exactly as planned, another problem in life will come up that competes for your attention, the task will get frustrating or complicated—the possibilities are endless. That's why we want to provide you with some general guidelines for approaching problems. Often, people who hoard get derailed by things that come up. They find them overwhelming, don't know what to do, have difficulty making decisions, and so on. To prevent this from happening to you, try the following steps:

1. Identify and define the problem. The trick here is to be as clear and specific as possible. What exactly is the problem you are facing? Here are some examples of well-defined and poorly defined problems:

Poorly defined problem	Well-defined problem
"My life has gotten out of control."	"I have too many demands on my time and I can't do them all."
"I just can't do this program."	"I'm having a hard time focusing on the book and remembering what it says."
"I'm just not well enough."	"I have diabetes, and when my blood sugar gets too low, I feel groggy and fatigued."
"There just isn't enough space in this place for me to spread out and get stuff organized."	"I need to find a way to sort my things in my little apartment."

2. Come up with as many solutions as possible. At this stage of problem-solving, the goal is to brainstorm and come up with lots of ideas, rather than evaluate them critically. Feel free to be creative and silly; that helps keep your thinking flexible. If you feel comfortable, ask a friend to help you think of things you might not have thought of yourself. Helen identified one of her problems as having too many demands on her time. Here's a list of possible solutions she brainstormed:

- *Make a list of priorities and decide which things are most important.*
- *Cancel some less-important activities that I have planned.*
- *Run off to Timbuktu.*
- *Ask a friend or family member to help me with some tasks so they'll go more quickly.*

3. Evaluate possible solutions and select the one or two that seem most reasonable and practical. Once you have generated a list of possibilities (which might include some silly ones), think about each one. Does it make sense? Is it feasible? Is it a good idea? Helen could see right off the bat that running off to Timbuktu was probably not a great long-term solution to her problems, so she crossed that off the list. However, the others seemed like they might be good ideas. At this stage in her program, she was still feeling a little shy about asking others for help, so she decided not to use that strategy right away. The other two, making a list of priorities and deciding which are most important, and canceling some less-important activities, sounded reasonable to her. She opted to go with those.

4. Implement the solution. After you've decided which solutions you're going to try, the next step is to actually do them: just thinking about solutions won't actually solve the problem. Helen sat down with a piece of paper and a pencil and wrote down a list of all the things that required her time. She then ordered them in terms of importance by putting a number next to each one. The items at the top of her list were those that she considered most important; those at the bottom of her list were the ones she considered optional. As she looked at the list, she decided that life would still go on even if she didn't accomplish all of those tasks. For example, she had previously agreed to answer phones for a political campaign as a volunteer. She decided that the sun would still come up the next day even if she didn't get that done, and that perhaps her time was better spent doing other things. She called the campaign office and canceled her shift. The mild guilt she felt was better than feeling overwhelmed and even more guilty about not doing other things she cared about more.

5. Evaluate the outcome. Once you have tried out your solution, determine whether it worked. Was it was helpful, neutral, or harmful? After she canceled her volunteer shift at the campaign office, Helen found that she now had several hours free to work on her hoarding. She got quite a bit done and concluded that canceling less-important activities was very helpful indeed. Had Helen instead found that the solution was neutral or even harmful to her, she would have gone back to her list of possible solutions and tried a different one.

Strategies for Sorting and Organizing

Make Categories

Before you begin sorting and organizing, decide on some basic categories that you will use. You will be putting possessions in piles, based on these categories. At the most basic level, begin by categorizing items as "things to keep" or "things to let go of." Let's start with the things you will let go of. What will you do with them? Everyone's answers might be a little different, but here are some good general categories that a lot of people have used:

Begin by categorizing items as "things to keep" or "things to let go of."

- Trash
- Things to recycle
- Things to give away (for example, to charities, a library, friends, or family)
- Things to sell (for example, yard sale, bookstore, consignment shop, Internet sales)

Next, let's think of categories for the things you want to save. Remember from Chapter 2 that many people who hoard have difficulty with this step. They tend to create too many categories, treating each item as if it were so special that it couldn't possibly be grouped with other items, even though other people would probably put them together. It will be important, therefore, to limit the number of categories you use. If your list has more than, say, 30 categories, you need to rethink your list. Are there categories that can be combined? For example, "sneakers" and "dress shoes" probably don't need their own categories; they could be grouped together under the more general category of "shoes." Here's the list of categories that Helen came up with.

Limit the number of categories you use.

Helen's Category List

1. *Mail & miscellaneous paper*
2. *Magazines*
3. *Photos*
4. *Clothing*
5. *Coats*
6. *Boots & shoes*
7. *Books*
8. *Audio & videotapes*
9. *Souvenirs*

10. *Decorative items*	20. *Linens*
11. *Gifts*	21. *Toiletries*
12. *Office supplies*	22. *Cleaning products*
13. *Games*	23. *Cleaning tools*
14. *Hardware*	24. *Garden & yard tools*
15. *Furniture*	25. *Recreation equipment*
16. *Storage containers*	26. *Paint & equipment*
17. *Food*	27. *Pet food & equipment*
18. *Kitchen utensils*	28. *Handicrafts*
19. *Pots, pans, dishes*	

Now you try it. Make a list of the categories of things you think you would like to save. If you just want to borrow Helen's list, that's fine (she won't mind). You can always revise your list once you start working. Remember, though, as is true with all of the exercises in this book, we want you to actually get a pencil or pen and write your responses down. Just reading about it won't help much, and trying to keep everything in your head will probably just overwhelm you and detract from what you're doing.

My Category List

1. _____	11. _____
2. _____	12. _____
3. _____	13. _____
4. _____	14. _____
5. _____	15. _____
6. _____	16. _____
7. _____	17. _____
8. _____	18. _____
9. _____	19. _____
10. _____	20. _____

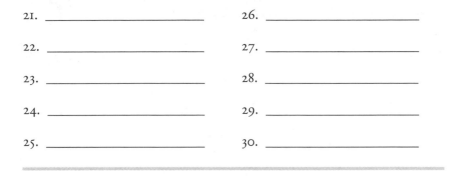

21. _____   26. _____

22. _____   27. _____

23. _____   28. _____

24. _____   29. _____

25. _____   30. _____

Decide on the Location for Each Category of Saved Items

Decide, up front, where things should go. Don't worry about doing this perfectly; no one could ever know where every single thing belongs. But we would like you to have some general ideas about where things go, so that you'll know where to put things once you start sorting and organizing. Because you will be sorting and organizing rapidly, you're not necessarily going to put every single item exactly where it belongs right away. For now, try to get things close enough to their proper locations, and then come back to the sorting and organizing task. You will probably also find that the task goes more quickly if, instead of putting everything where it belongs right when you find it, you prepare some cardboard boxes or plastic bins for each of the categories, and write the category name on the box. After a half an hour or so of sorting, put the items in each box where they belong. Watch out for the trap of leaving the boxes where they are and saying, "I'll get to those eventually." Do not end a sorting and organizing session without putting away all the items that you have sorted.

> *Do not end a sorting and organizing session without putting away all items that you have sorted.*

Helen wrote down where she thought each category (from the list above) should go. Here's her list:

☞ Helen's Categories and Locations

Categories for Saving	Locations for Saving
1. *Mail & miscellaneous paper*	*File cabinets, drawers, processing pile*
2. *Magazines*	*Shelves*

Categories for Saving	Locations for Saving
3. *Photos*	*Boxes*
4. *Clothing*	*Drawers, closets, laundry basket*
5. *Coats*	*Closet*
6. *Boots & shoes*	*Shoe rack*
7. *Books*	*Shelves*
8. *Audio & videotapes*	*Shelves*
9. *Souvenirs*	*Display cabinets, storage*
10. *Decorative items*	*On display, storage*
11. *Gifts*	*Storage*
12. *Office supplies*	*Desk drawer, top of desk*
13. *Games*	*Cabinets*
14. *Hardware*	*Garage*
15. *Furniture*	*Placed in room, storage*
16. *Empty containers*	*Cupboards, basement*
17. *Food*	*Refrigerator, pantry*
18. *Kitchen utensils*	*Drawers*
19. *Pots, pans, dishes*	*Cupboards*
20. *Linens*	*Linen closet*
21. *Toiletries*	*Bathroom cabinet*
22. *Cleaning products*	*Kitchen cabinet*
23. *Cleaning tools*	*Closet*
24. *Garden & yard tools*	*Garage*
25. *Recreation equipment*	*Garage*
26. *Paint & equipment*	*Basement*
27. *Pet food & equipment*	*Closet*
28. *Handicrafts*	*Basement*

Your possessions might not be exactly like Helen's, and your home may not have the same kind of spaces hers does. So we'd like you to try this yourself, with your own categories and the spaces in your home.

Categories for Saving

Locations for Storage

1. _____   _____

2. _____   _____

3. _____   _____

4. _____   _____

5. _____   _____

6. _____   _____

7. _____   _____

8. _____   _____

9. _____   _____

10. _____   _____

11. _____   _____

12. _____   _____

13. _____   _____

14. _____   _____

15. _____   _____

16. _____   _____

17. _____   _____

18. _____   _____

19. _____   _____

20. _____   _____

21. _____   _____

22. _____   _____

23. _____   _____

Categories for Saving	*Locations for Storage*
24. _____	_____
25. _____	_____
26. _____	_____
27. _____	_____
28. _____	_____
29. _____	_____
30. _____	_____

A general decision-making plan is depicted in Figure 9.2. During a sorting and organizing session, you will pick up each item in front of you, one at a time, and make a decision about whether you want to keep it or remove it from your home. If you decide to remove it (the left side of the diagram), determine whether it is something to throw away, recycle, give away, or sell. Having made that decision, take the item to its proper location. For example, if you decide that the item is trash, put it in an appropriate trash container such as a wastebasket, garbage can, or dumpster. If the item is to be recycled, put it in a recycling bin or a box for pickup or to take to the local

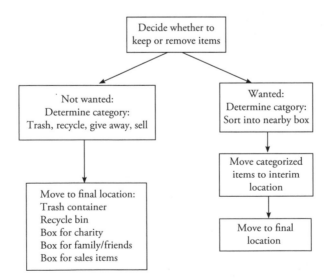

Figure 9.2 A General Decision-Making Plan

recycling center. You should also designate boxes for things to be donated, given away, or sold, and put items in their respective boxes as you go.

If, on the other hand, you decide to keep the item (the right side of the diagram), decide what category it goes in using your list from earlier in this chapter. If you have designated cardboard boxes for each of the categories, put each item in the appropriate box. If you don't have enough boxes yet for all of the categories, it's OK to create small piles of items for each category; just make sure the piles don't get too big, and that you put them away as you finish the sorting session and make a plan to get the boxes or bins you need. If you're planning on keeping a large number of items, it might be helpful to select a "staging area" nearby to hold things until you're ready to put them away. Again, however, make sure that by the end of the session, everything has gone to its final location according to the list you made above. For some things, you might need a temporary storage location if the clutter prevents you from putting it where it belongs.

Finding Your Local Recycling Center

Most cities or towns provide bins for curbside recycling or have a center that accepts recyclable materials. They vary in what kinds of materials they will accept, so it's a good idea to look this up on the Internet or call first. If you have difficulty locating your recycling center, you can look it up at www.earth911.com. This Web site also offers lots of useful information about how to recycle appropriately. In addition, more and more cities and towns are offering curbside pickup of recyclables.

Charities That Will Pick Up

Note: These charities are listed for your convenience only. Their listing here does not constitute an endorsement of any charitable organization or cause.

American Lung Association (cars only): www.donateyourcar.org

Cristina Foundation (computers only): (203) 863-9100 or www.cristina.org

Donate a Car 2 Charity (cars only): 1-877-505-5775 or www.donateacar2charity.com

Donation Line (cars only): 1-877-227-7487 or www.donationline.com

Freecycle: www.freecycle.org

Goodwill: (301) 530-6500 or http://locator.goodwill.org/

Salvation Army: 1-800-95-TRUCK or www.salvationarmy.org

Society of St. Vincent de Paul: (314) 576-3993 or www.svdpusa.org/

(continued)

As you might imagine, for sorting and organizing to really succeed, you're going to have to do some prep work in advance. Everyone's situation is a little different, but here are some general suggestions:

- Make sure you have boxes or storage containers for the things you want to keep. You'll also need boxes or other suitable containers for things to be recycled, donated, or sold. Some recycling centers, consignment shops, or other places may have specific requirements for how items should be packaged or bundled; be sure to check in advance.

- If you're going to have a lot of boxes of things to keep, you'll need to get labels so that you will know what's in each box without having to open it. You will also need a pen or marker to write on the labels. Alternatively, clear plastic containers can be helpful for determining the contents of a box at a glance, although labels are still very important for sorting and easily finding what you are looking for.

- Have a large supply of garbage bags for trash.

- Have recycle bins for recycling materials.

- If you have a very large amount of clutter and plan to get rid of a lot of it, consider renting a dumpster. Many independent trash-hauling companies or home stores (see your Yellow Pages) will deliver a dumpster to your home and pick it up when you're done.

- You might also find it helpful to identify someone who can help you. Sorting and organizing is a big task and can be quite time-consuming, with a fair amount of physical labor involved. If you have a trusted friend or family member who can help, or a neighborhood high school or college student who is trustworthy and reliable, now is the time to contact that person. Many colleges have a student work office where you can hire someone by the hour. Alternatively, some independent trash-hauling or moving companies can send someone to your home, for a fee, to help you carry things.

- Clear some space to work. Once you start sorting and organizing, you are going to have to move things around. This means that things might actually get messier before they get cleaner. If possible, designate a "staging area" somewhere near where you will be working. If there is simply too much clutter to create a staging area, try creating one in an outside hallway, porch, or yard. Remember, things will go there only temporarily and you will clear out the staging area by the end of the session.

- Schedule times for working. Our experience tells us quite clearly that you will get the best results when you schedule a specific time for sorting and organizing. Doing this "once in a while," "when I get to it," or "here and there throughout the day" doesn't seem to work very well. Use the calendar from earlier in this chapter to help figure out the best time to work.

Below you will find a form to help you list things you need to do to make your sorting and organizing sessions go smoothly. Copy this form so that you can use it for each room in the house. For rooms that have a lot of clutter or a complex layout, you might need to use multiple forms within a single room. Here is an example of a form that Bill completed before his first sorting and organizing session:

●✎ Bill's Preparing for Organizing Form

Room: *Living room*

Target Area or Type of Object: *Area around entertainment center*

Things I need to do to prepare for organizing:

1. *Rent a dumpster and have it delivered.*
2. *Get a box of plastic garbage bags.*
3. *Bring cardboard boxes up from the basement.*

4. *Buy labels and marker.*
5. *Clear a temporary staging area elsewhere in the room.*
6. *Call my daughter and ask her to come over and help.*

Now it's your turn. Pick a room in the house, and write down the things you will need to do in order to make sorting and organizing a success. You will repeat this process for the different rooms in your home. If you have clutter outside your home as well, think about what you will need to do for that area as well.

➥ My Preparing for Organizing Form

Room: _____

Target Area or Type of Object: _____

Things I need to do to prepare for organizing:

1. _____

2. _____

3. _____

4. _____

5. _____

6. _____

✳ Special Considerations for Paper Items

Many of the people we have talked to who hoard tell us that they have particular difficulty deciding what to do about paper items such as mail, newspapers and magazines, personal documents, and so on. As a result, people who hoard often mix important and unimportant things, so checks and bills get mixed with grocery store fliers and newspapers. This makes it extremely difficult to deal with clutter effectively: if piles of useless paper might contain something important, you then have to go through them more carefully (and more slowly) than you would if important papers were put away properly. It is crucial to set up a filing system for bills and documents, as well as places to store other papers such as informational materials, upcoming events, travel information, pictures, and so forth. Establishing a filing system early on helps with the sorting of items in each room.

The idea of putting important papers out of sight might make you nervous. Many people who hoard are worried that if they put things out of sight, they will forget about them. Remember, the goal of this task is to create usable living space and to be able to find things you need easily. You have probably noticed that it's hard

It is crucial to set up a filing system for bills and documents.

to find things in piles. By creating an efficient filing system, you will know where important things are without having to actually have them in sight.

You will probably find it helpful to get a small filing cabinet or other filing system, available in most furniture or office-supply stores. Even a cardboard box will do. Create a separate file for different kinds of paper items. Here are some general categories to get you started; feel free to revise this list to meet your specific needs.

➡ General Categories for Filing Paper

- Addresses and phone numbers
- Articles you want to read, cut out from newspapers and magazines
- Automobile
- Catalogs
- Computer
- Correspondence
- Coupons
- Entertainment
- Financial (credit cards, bank statements, retirement account, savings account, checking account, stocks or other investments)
- Humor
- Individuals (by name): One file for each household member
- Instruction manuals/warranties
- Medical
- Personal documents (wills, insurance policies, etc.)

- Photographs (this is a temporary file; eventually, photographs should be put in a photo album or other appropriate place)
- Product information
- Restaurants
- School papers
- Sentimental items
- Services
- Stamps
- Stationery
- Taxes
- Things-to-do lists
- Things to file (things that have to be reviewed)
- Calendar items (reminders for that specific month)
- Trips/vacation information

◗✦ Things I Need to Get for Filing Paper

1. _____

2. _____

3. _____

4. _____

Suggested items:

- File folders
- Hanging files
- Filing cabinets
- Labels
- Desk organizer

Often, it's hard to know how long to hang on to paper items. Not everything needs to be saved forever. Here are some general recommendations:

Keep for 1 Month

Not everything needs to be saved forever.

- Credit-card receipts
- Sales receipts for minor purchases
- Withdrawal and deposit slips. Toss after you've checked them against your monthly bank statement.

Keep for 1 Year

- Paycheck stubs/direct deposit receipts
- Monthly bank, credit-card, brokerage, mutual-fund, and retirement-account statements

Keep for 6 Years

- W-2's, 1099s, and other material for your tax returns
- Year-end credit-card statements, brokerage and mutual-fund summaries

Keep Indefinitely

- Tax returns
- Receipts for major purchases (such as furniture)
- Real estate and residence records
- Wills and trusts

Keep in a Safe-Deposit Box

- Birth and death certificates
- Marriage licenses
- Insurance policies
- Automobile titles
- Property deeds

Putting Items in Their Designated Locations So They Are Easily Located in the Future

Regular upkeep is key to keeping clutter under control, particularly when it comes to paper items. As you might recall, Helen was particularly troubled by the amount of mail that came in every day, so she created a filing system right there in her kitchen, where she normally dropped her mail. Each day, after getting her mail, she sorted it into one of three categories: trash (which went in the garbage can), recycle (which went in the recycle bin), or keep (which went into a small box on the counter to be dealt with at her convenience). She deliberately chose a small box so that she would not be able to put off dealing with those items indefinitely. At least once a week, she would go through the box and empty it out, paying bills that needed to be paid and filing any other items she wanted to keep.

Newspapers and magazines also require regular upkeep. If you're having difficulty keeping up with reading them, consider canceling subscriptions to periodicals you haven't read in the past 6 months. Many newspapers can be delivered once a week rather than every day, or even read online for free. If you decide that there is something you want to read, rather than saving the entire newspaper or magazine, cut out the article and file it for later reading. Here's one Web site with information about how to reduce junk mail: http://www.privacyrights.org/fs/fs4-junk.htm.

Regular upkeep is key to keeping clutter under control, particularly when it comes to paper items.

Create a routine so that uncluttering becomes a habit. Here are some general suggestions that we have found useful:

- Pick a time to sort new mail and papers every day.
- Incorporate some recreational time into each day after sorting to boost your spirits and reward yourself.
- Empty your trash twice weekly (more often if required).
- Take the trash out for pickup (or deliver to sanitation facilities) at the same time every week.
- Do dishes daily so you wake up to a clean sink and counter.
- Do laundry every week (more often if required).

- Establish times and a system for paying bills to meet due dates.
- Put all new purchases away upon arrival, or at least within the same day.
- Put away any used items as soon as the task is done.

A professional organizer friend of ours gave us the suggestions listed here. Consider copying this list and putting it on your refrigerator door with a magnet:

- If you take it out, put it back.
- If you open it, close it.
- If you throw it down, pick it up.
- If you take it off, hang it up.
- If you use it, clean it up.

Reward Yourself

At times, sorting and organizing can feel like a lot of work, and we admit it's not particularly exciting (although we hope, as you get into it, you will feel good about the progress you're making). To keep your motivation high, it's helpful to build rewards into your program. Take a moment and think about what you like to do: Watch TV? Go for walks? Talk on the telephone? Eat ice cream? Play with a pet? Whatever it is, make it an important part of your sorting and organizing sessions. After you have worked on your hoarding problem for the designated period of time (perhaps 30 minutes), reward yourself by doing the thing you like. But there's a catch to this: you should reward yourself only *after you have sorted and organized for the designated amount of time.* Otherwise, the reward will not be associated with the work and will become meaningless. Take a moment to write down how you intend to reward yourself:

To keep your motivation high, it's helpful to build rewards into your program.

➦ My Rewards

After _____ minutes of sorting and organizing, I will reward myself in one or more of the following ways:

1. _____

2. _____

3. _____

I agree to reward myself consistently, so I get rewarded each time I achieve my sorting and organizing goal. I also agree *not* to give myself these rewards until I meet my daily goal.

In the next chapter, we will walk you through the actual steps of sorting and organizing. Be sure that you have done the appropriate prep work before you go on.

IO

Sorting/Removing Stuff
Let's Go!

 Motivation Booster

In this chapter you will begin your sorting and organizing sessions, applying what you learned in Chapter 5. You will also begin the task of learning how to let go of things that are keeping you from reaching your goals. Before we start, however, you need to take a moment and revisit your Practice Muscle. By now, you should have exercised your Practice Muscle enough so that you can work for 30 minutes at a stretch on sorting and removing things. If not, back up to Chapter 5 (page 58) and review the steps. You must get yourself to the point where you can work for 30 to 60 minutes each day. Unless you do, it is unlikely that you can achieve your goals. You can do it. It might help to review your goals and values to make sure they are consistent with the program. Go back to these every day as you spend time practicing sorting and letting go.

"For every minute spent in organizing, an hour is earned"—Benjamin Franklin

My most important goals are: *My most important values are:*

1. _____   _____

2. _____   _____

3. _____   _____

Let's go back and review.

As you have no doubt discovered by now, letting go of your stuff can lead to distressing feelings of anxiety, uncertainty, guilt, and regret. Experiencing these emotions sometimes leads people to save possessions they should get rid of. To get control over your hoarding, you must learn to tolerate these feelings. In the same way that you strengthened your Practice Muscle, you can learn to tolerate these unpleasant emotions. All you need is practice. If you find them hindering your progress, start out getting rid of things that cause only mild distress and work your way up to more challenging types of items.

✳ Where Do I Start?

You may have already answered this question while you were learning about getting ready in the last chapter. If not, then you'll want to think about beginning with a location that offers you several things. First, you want to start with someplace that will have an impact on your day-to-day life. This might be the entrance to your home, a hallway, kitchen, living room, and so forth. You want the clearing you do to be noticed every day and to allow you more freedom of movement and use of the space. Second, you might want to think a step or two ahead. Perhaps clearing a space on a table or couch would allow you to sit during sorting and letting-go sessions and would make the whole process easier. If all else fails in trying to find the best place to start, you can always just begin with the first place that catches your eye, or even wherever you are right now as you read this! Wherever you start, it is important to stick with it until the area is clear.

Wherever you start, it is important to stick with it until the area is clear.

Avoid the trap of working on one area for a few minutes, then going to another area. Sticking with the area where you start until it is cleared will allow you to see the progress you have made and will go a long way toward keeping your motivation high.

Once you've picked a place to start, you must pick a time. Pick a time during the day when you are at your best. Recall that Bill felt "sharper" in the mornings and selected mornings as his best time to work. Begin with a 30-minute session, and schedule one each day. What is most important at this point is that you stick to this schedule, regardless of how you feel or what else is going on in your life. That means giving this work highest priority. We can predict with some certainty that in the time leading up to your scheduled 30 minutes, all sorts of things will be going on that will make you want to put it off or not do it at all. Each of these things will seem legitimate, and a decision to put off your 30 minutes will seem perfectly reasonable. You must be ready to resist this tendency. It will be your major obstacle to making progress on this problem!

For your first sorting session, make sure you have the materials you need (see Chapter 9), especially your list of categories and locations. If you will be working with paper, have your filing categories and file folders handy.

Each sorting session should follow roughly the same procedure. You will pick something up in the area where you are working, and you will make three decisions about it, followed by an action (see Fig. 9.2):

Decision 1: Should I keep it or let go of it?

Decision 2: To what category does this thing belong?

Decision 3: Where should it go?

Action: Move the item to its final location.

Before reading any further, let's try it. Pick up something, make these three decisions, and move the item to its final location.

OK, now how did it go? What were the complications? Write them here.

✎ Complications:

1. _____

2. _____

3. _____

The complications you experienced with this sorting task are the things we will spend the most time on in the next few chapters. Solving these complications will require some creativity on your part. The more sorting and letting-go sessions you have, the easier this will get.

✳ Decision: Keep or Let Go?

In the last chapter you learned how to prepare for and make the second and third decisions in the sorting/letting-go sessions. The first decision—whether or not to keep it—will be our focus for most of this chapter. Please remember that you are the one to make this decision. In this book we will not try to tell you what you should or should not keep; that decision is yours. We are more concerned with your ability to make that decision in such a way that you can achieve the goals you have laid out for yourself in Chapter 7.

Decision-Making Questions

Frequently we find that people who have trouble controlling their possessions keep things without thinking much about them. Recall from our previous chapters that this avoids the unpleasant experiences associated with getting rid of things. It's easier just to keep it for a later time or "just in case" it might be needed later. To counteract this process, begin by picking up an item and simply describing aloud your thoughts about it. After you've spent a few minutes doing this, make a decision about whether to keep or let go of it. Try it now with any object that you can reach from where you sit.

As you do this, you may find that the decision becomes clear. After you've done this a few times, jot down the major themes or questions that helped you make that decision. Below are some examples that our clients have found helpful. Fill in the blanks with your own.

- How many do I already have, and is that enough?
- Do I have enough time to actually use, review, or read it?
- Have I used this in the past year?
- Do I have a specific plan to use this item within a reasonable timeframe?
- Does this fit with my own values and needs?
- How does this compare with the things I value highly?
- Does this seem important just because I'm looking at it now?
- Is it current?
- Is it of good quality, accurate, and/or reliable?

- Is it easy to understand?
- Would I buy it again if I didn't already own it?
- Do I really need it?
- Could I get it again if I found I really needed it?
- Do I have enough space for this?
- Will not having this help me solve my hoarding problem?
- _____
- _____
- _____
- _____
- _____

You will find that refining the questions will speed up your decision-making. As you get more practice, you'll be able to "zero in" on the specific questions that work best for you; then you won't have to ask yourself every single one of our questions. Before going on, make the second and third decisions for the items you've practiced on and put them in their final location.

Rules for Letting Go of Things

In addition to using the questions above, another way to gain control over what you keep is to establish a few simple rules for deciding what to keep and what to get rid of. For example, you might establish a rule for newspapers that if they are more than a week old, you will recycle them regardless of whether or not they have been read. For magazines, you might set the same rule at a month instead of a week. Or you might establish a rule for clothes that if you haven't worn them or been able to fit into them for a year, they should be donated to a charity. Having these rules will greatly simplify your life, make your decisions much easier, and allow you to reach the goals you've laid out for yourself. Take a moment right now and write down a set of rules for keeping and getting rid of things. If you can't figure out just the right rules, make a few guesses and use them for a week to see if they work for you. You can always adjust them. Even if you make mistakes and get rid of a few things you might regret, in the long run the loss will be worth it since you will discover what rules are best for you.

1. _____

2. _____

3. _____

4. _____

5. _____

6. _____

The OHIO Rule

You've probably had the experience of picking something up, trying to figure out whether to keep it, how long to keep it, where to put it, and so on—and in the end you just put it back where you found it. We've seen this phenomenon often enough in people's attempts to clear their clutter that we refer to it as "churning." Things are picked up and examined, but they simply go back onto the pile without any decisions being made about them. To try to get over this problem, we recommend the *OHIO rule: "Only Handle It Once."* The idea is that once you pick something up, you should decide whether to keep or get rid of it, and if you keep it, you should put it away where it belongs and not back onto the pile. In reality, handling things only once is not always possible since the final destination for things may not be available. However, it is possible to reduce "churning" by making a decision and formulating a plan for where the object is to go in the meantime.

OHIO rule: "Only Handle It Once."

✳ Following Through

There are two basic steps in effective decision-making. The first is to make a decision, and the second is to follow through with it. Once you have made a decision to keep or let go of a possession, it is critical that you follow through with the other decisions and the final action immediately. You may have experienced this as a complication with your first sorting task above. One of the most common problems in the homes of people with out-of-control clutter is that even after they make a decision to let go of something, it sits by the door or in the car for so long that the person no longer trusts his or her decision and has to think about it all over again before feeling comfortable letting go. If you make the decision to let go of something, you must decide on its category (to discard, recycle, donate, or sell), decide where it should go, and get it there right away. On the other hand, if you make a decision to keep something, it is equally important that you select its category and location using the plan you made in Chapter 9. Then, get that item to a destination that is out of the way and not contributing to the clutter. If your home is very cluttered, you'll need to decide on an interim destination. The key is to move the item from the middle of the living area to an appropriate area that is out of the way.

Tolerating Distress

If you're like most people with hoarding problems, the process of sorting/ removing stuff is going to be uncomfortable. You might have emotional reactions like sadness, anxiety, guilt, or anger. You might experience a lot of thoughts about responsibility, perfection, or identity. You might feel a sense of grief and loss that comes from excessive emotional attachment to possessions. Recognize that these reactions are all fine, and although they feel bad, none of them need to get in your way. Sometimes when we're talking to people about hoarding, we get a question like, "But what am I supposed to do when I feel anxious?" Sometimes the best answer is: nothing. Sometimes your emotions just need to be tolerated, rather than fixed. A lot of the time our urge to "fix" our feelings comes from a worry that these feelings will stick around for a very long time, or that they will get worse and worse, or that they will cause our functioning to break down in some way. Often, these predictions aren't accurate, as we'll discuss below. So as you notice yourself feeling emotionally distressed, try acknowledging the feeling without acting on it. You can feel anxious, sad, or angry, *and* keep going.

Experimenting With Letting Go

So far in this chapter we have discussed strategies for improving the effectiveness of your sorting and letting-go decisions. Now we come to a much harder task: examining the basis for your decisions to save so many things. We cannot tell you which possessions you should keep and which ones you should get rid of. However, our experience with this problem has shown us that often, people's beliefs about their things are out of sync with how they want to live, but these beliefs have never been closely examined or evaluated. In the next few chapters we will help you develop ways to examine these beliefs and make them more consistent with your goals and values in life. This is the part of your program that will be the most stressful and difficult, because to evaluate your beliefs, you have to experiment with getting rid of things you would not ordinarily discard. You will have to risk not having something when you need it, getting rid of things you like, and so forth.

The purpose of this experiment is not to get rid of your stuff or to declutter, but to learn what is most important to you and how to change your perspective about the things you own. We are suggesting that you become a scientist studying a very important subject: you. So what does a scientist actually do? Almost all scientific activities can be boiled down to two main steps. First, a scientist makes a *prediction* about something, like, "If I mix chemical X with chemical Y, the result will be an explosion." Next, the scientist *tests* that prediction by actually doing the action to see if the prediction came true. So the scientist actually mixes chemical X with chemical Y to see whether the mixture explodes (in this case, for the scientist's sake, we hope the prediction was not true!). So we'd like you to try the same process. First, you have to come up with a prediction, and second, you have to test it to see if the prediction comes true.

Let's try a simple one. Pick something like a newspaper, magazine, piece of clothing you haven't worn in years, an empty container, or anything of the sort. Write what it is in the space below. Now answer the following question: How would you feel if you let go of this thing? That means right now, before you've had a chance to read it, wear it, use it, and so forth. Write how you would feel on the line below. Also, try to rate how bad (distressing, depressing, anxiety-provoking, etc.) that would be on a scale from 0 (not at all) to 10 (unbearable).

What is the item you identified? _____

How would it feel to let go of this item? _____

How bad would that feeling be? _____ (0–10)

How long would it take to get over that feeling? _____

What bad outcome would happen if you let go of the item?

_____

How difficult would it be for you to recover if that bad thing happened?
_____ (0–10)

You have just made several important predictions about your attachment to objects. We can now state the prediction as, "If I let go of this object, I will feel _____," "On a 10-point scale, the strength of my feeling will be _____," "It would take _____ amount of time for me to get over that feeling," "If I let go of this object, the following bad outcome will happen...," and "If that bad thing happened, it would be _____ (on a 10-point scale) difficult for me to recover."

We asked Helen to try this exercise. Here's what she wrote:

What item did you identify? *Credit-card advertisement*

How would it feel to let go of this item? *Scary*

How bad would that feeling be? (0–10) *9*

How long would it take to get over that feeling? *I would never get over it*

What bad outcome would happen if you let go of the item?
I would need a new credit card and I wouldn't have the right information.

How difficult would it be for you to recover if that bad thing happened? (0–10) *8*

So, are you ready to test your predictions? Remember, to learn about your attachments to possessions, you are going to have to experience unpleasant things. This experiment will tell you whether your assumptions about how bad it would be are accurate. Put the item you've identified into the trash (or recycling, etc.) and get it out of the house so it is clear that getting rid of it is final. Do it right now before reading any further. Come back to this spot in the book.

Now write below how you feel.

I feel _____.

My distress rating (0–10) is _____.

Was it as bad as you expected? If you are like most people, you probably anticipated something worse than what actually happened. If it was as bad as you expected, or worse, the experience can lead you to examine these feelings more closely. Some of the approaches described in the next chapter can help. You might want to write down your observations about this experiment and what you have learned so far.

To complete the experiment, rate how you feel about getting rid of this object on the scale of 0 to 10 each day for the next week.

Day 1: _____ Day 2: _____ Day 3: _____ Day 4: _____

Day 5: _____ Day 6: _____ Day 7: _____

At the end of the week, give some thought to what this means. If you are no longer bothered by not having this thing, what does that tell you about your original attachment to it? If you are still upset about losing it, let's examine those feelings closely as you read through the next few chapters.

One of the things we know about anxiety and distress, particularly of this sort, is that over time it goes away or lessens. You can use that process (which psychologists call "habituation") to change the way you feel about your possessions. By simply putting up with the distress for a period of time, you start to feel better. The distress goes away, you become stronger, and you don't feel as bad the next time. In fact, you can do this in a very structured way by creating a list or "hierarchy" of items to let go of

Getting rid of the easiest items first builds up your tolerance and makes it easier when you get to the harder items later on.

that starts with easier items and works up to the hardest ones. Getting rid of the easiest items first builds up your tolerance and makes it easier when you get to the harder items later on. Try filling in this form and then start with the items lowest on the hierarchy.

	Item to let go of	Distress rating for letting go of this item (0–10)
1.	_____	_____
2.	_____	_____
3.	_____	_____
4.	_____	_____
5.	_____	_____
6.	_____	_____
7.	_____	_____
8.	_____	_____
9.	_____	_____
10.	_____	_____

With each sorting and letting-go session, you should be testing out your assumptions like a scientist. Testing-it-out exercises can be set up in all sorts of ways. The exercises you come up with should be guided by what you learned about yourself in Chapter 6. For instance, if a major reason you save newspapers is because you think you can't afford to miss what was in them and that doing so will somehow change your life dramatically, check it out by throwing away a newspaper and keep track of how much it changed your life during the following week. Go over the results carefully to determine whether your life has changed dramatically for the worse.

Below is a form you can use to create your own testing-it-out exercises. Remember, the key here is that you are learning something about your relationship to the things you save and whether your beliefs about your things are really accurate.

1. Testing-it-out exercise to be completed: _____

   _____

   _____

2. What do you predict (are afraid) will happen? _____

   _____

   _____

3. How strongly do you believe this will happen (0–100 percent)?

   _____

4. Initial discomfort (0–10) _____

5. What actually happened? _____

   _____

   _____

6. Final discomfort (0—10) _____

7. Did your predictions come true? _____

   _____

8. What conclusions do you draw from this exercise? _____

   _____

   _____

To recap what we have covered in this chapter, your daily sorting and letting-go sessions should last at least 30 minutes. During that time you should apply what you have learned about organizing in Chapter 9, and making decisions, following through, and running experiments and exercises in this chapter. This will not always go smoothly. You will undoubtedly run into problems, mostly the "bad guys." Learn how to cope with them in the next chapter.

Your daily sorting and letting-go sessions should last at least 30 minutes.

Here Come the Bad Guys
Part 1. Motivation and Working Time

Remember the five bad guys from Chapter 4? We bet that one or more of them will show up (if they haven't already) at some point during your sorting and organizing sessions. Perhaps, once you started sorting and organizing, you found yourself feeling less invested in the process, or other tasks started competing for your time. Perhaps you started worrying that you were doing it wrong, or that you would let go of something important. Perhaps the whole thing started to feel overwhelming or confusing to you. Perhaps you noticed yourself starting to procrastinate or put it off. Or perhaps you just wanted to do things that felt easier or better. This is perfectly normal; in fact, nearly all of the people we've met with hoarding problems run into one or more of these problems somewhere along the way.

But don't worry; the good guys from Chapter 5 are on your side and can help you get through this. In the next two chapters, we'll discuss how each of the bad guys might show up, and how you can use the good guys to beat them.

Here's where it can get a little tricky. You don't necessarily have to read every part of this chapter or the next one; rather, you need to read only the sections that apply to the bad guys that are bothering you. Use the flowchart included here (Fig. 11.1) to determine which sections you need to read.

Bad Guy #1: "It's just not my priority"

If you find that other things start to seem more important to you than sorting and organizing, stop and reassess your goals and priorities. Are these other things true emergencies that you really must attend to right now?

Figure 11.1 Flowchart

Sometimes, that's what happens. A loved one might have to go to the hospital, the water tank might burst, you might lose your job and have to find a new one—things like this are time-limited crises, and you might well decide that you need to deal with them right away. If so, that's fine—the program will still be here when you're finished dealing with the crisis.

In other cases, however, it's less clear-cut. The things competing for your time and attention might not be *bona fide* emergencies, or they might be chronic situations that will continue to be there, perhaps indefinitely. Perhaps you have a chronic (but not necessarily completely debilitating) illness that needs to be treated or managed. Or perhaps you have a lot of family responsibilities, such as taking your children to school and soccer practice. Perhaps you have a job that requires you to work long hours. Perhaps there are other things you'd just rather be doing. We certainly understand that these kinds of situations can make it hard for you to stay motivated and keep going with your sorting and organizing. And we'd like you to try to see that these things need not get in the way of your progress. Even very, very busy people can find sufficient time to succeed with this program.

Even very, very busy people can find sufficient time to succeed with this program.

Keeping Your Eyes on the Prize

Go back to Chapter 7 and look at your values and personal goals for this program. Do you still have those same goals today? If you are feeling ambivalent, is it because your goals have truly changed, or is it because you have stopped keeping those goals in mind? Also look at what you wrote about the likely consequences of working on hoarding versus not working on hoarding. Do these consequences still seem likely? Now look at the contract you made with yourself. Are you still willing to honor it? You might even find it helpful to post a copy of it somewhere visible, like on your refrigerator or bathroom mirror. If you can be reminded of your goals on a daily basis, this will help keep them at the front of your mind.

Let's try the clutter and unclutter visualization exercises again. Go to the room where you had been working and noticed your motivation starting to fade. Try the exercise, writing your answers in the spaces provided.

➤ Clutter Visualization Exercise

Room: _____

A. Look around the room, noticing the clutter. Turn slowly so you can see all of it.

B. How uncomfortable did you feel while looking around this room? Circle a number on the scale below:

0   1   2   3   4   5   6   7   8   9   10

no discomfort   severe discomfort

C. What feelings were you having while looking around this room?

1. _____

2. _____

3. _____

D. What thoughts or beliefs were you having while looking around this room?

1. _____

2. _____

3. _____

A. Now visualize this room with the clutter gone (it might help to close your eyes when you do this). Imagine cleared surfaces and floors, tabletops without piles, and uncluttered floors with only rugs and furniture. For now, don't worry about where the things have gone; just imagine the room without clutter.

B. How uncomfortable did you feel while looking around this room? Circle a number on the scale below:

0	1	2	3	4	5	6	7	8	9	10

no discomfort   severe discomfort

C. What thoughts and feelings were you having while visualizing this room?

1. _____

2. _____

3. _____

D. Imagine what you can do in this room now that it is not cluttered. Picture how pleasant this room will feel when you have arranged it the way you want it. Describe your thoughts and feelings.

1. _____

2. _____

3. _____

E. How uncomfortable did you feel while imagining the room this way? Use the scale below:

0	1	2	3	4	5	6	7	8	9	10

no discomfort   severe discomfort

Sometimes, careful scheduling is required to keep you motivated and working at your best. In Chapter 9, you completed a daily and weekly calendar. Take another look at these; when would be a good time to schedule your sorting/organizing sessions? Try to find a time when you know you'll be mentally alert enough to do the task, and when you'll have the fewest other things competing for your time. Even if you have to get up a half-hour early to work on the clutter, you might find it worth your while.

It's also important to think about where beating hoarding fits into your priorities and values. Below, we'd like you to list the top priorities in your life. Write down as many as you can, including beating hoarding, then read on.

●← My Top Priorities

1. _____
2. _____
3. _____
4. _____
5. _____
6. _____

Where did beating hoarding rank on your list? If it ranked high, ask yourself: Am I letting lower-priority things interfere with beating hoarding? If, on the other hand, beating hoarding is ranked low, ask yourself: Are these other things really more important to me, or do they just seem that way because they're on my mind a lot? If you decide, after careful consideration, that beating hoarding is simply not high on your list of priorities, perhaps it would make sense to give yourself a break and not work on it right now. On the other hand, if beating hoarding really *is* important to you, then you will need to renew your commitment to work on the problem and stay on task.

Your Practice Muscle

Sometimes when we haven't been able to reach our goals, we give up and decide that the goal is unattainable. If that describes you, think carefully about why you haven't reached your goals. If you have not spent 30 to 60 minutes each and every day working on this problem, you aren't likely to reach your goals anytime soon. You are in luck, however, because you can change this. Go back to Chapter 6 and reread Good Guy #6. Start again to condition your Practice Muscle. Once you get up to 30 minutes each day, you will see progress.

Bad Guy #2: Avoidance and Excuse-Making

If you're like a lot of people who hoard, by now you may have already noticed yourself avoiding certain aspects of sorting/discarding, or perhaps making excuses to yourself or to others. Do any of these sound familiar?

- "I'm too tired to do this right now."
- "I just don't have enough energy."
- "I'm so busy I can't possibly find the time to sort."
- "I'm too stressed out to work on my hoarding problem."
- "I wouldn't be able to tolerate it if I felt bad."
- "What I really need is more space."

Let's start by acknowledging these statements for what they are: excuses that promote avoidance and ultimately undermine your ability to get on top of the problem. You are certainly not alone in thinking this way, but if you want to beat the hoarding problem, you are going to have to work through these excuses and confront things that are difficult.

Some of these statements can be categorized as "fatigue/low energy/ stress" excuses. Let's work on those first.

Your Practice Muscle

When you develop your Practice Muscle for sorting and discarding, you will be increasing your stamina or ability to work for long stretches of time. Remember, you can't increase your stamina by resting. Stamina and energy improve by progressively increasing your workload, such as in an exercise program. You start by exercising a little bit, then gradually work your way up to doing more and more. Each time, try to push yourself a little bit farther past the point where you become tired. This means continuing to work on your hoarding despite feeling tired, anxious, depressed, or even ill. Increase the amount of time you do this a little bit each day. Eventually, it will take you longer to tire out. By continuing to work on the hoarding problem a little bit at a time, you will gradually increase your energy level until you are able to go for long enough to make real progress.

What is your Practice Muscle Strength right now? If it is below 30, start working your way up slowly just as we discussed in Chapter 6.

Your Practice Muscle Strength

0	5	10	15	20	25	30	35	40	45	50	55	60

Minutes per day   Minutes per day

Thinking It Through

When we are feeling upset or emotionally vulnerable, it's common to underestimate our own ability. It's easier to say, "I can't" than to say, "Let me figure out how I can." Think about your own experience: have you ever been able to do something tough, even though you were feeling tired or stressed out? We'll bet you have. When we are determined and motivated, it's often amazing what we can accomplish.

Other excuses might be categorized as "emotional overload/perceived inability to cope." The emotion might be fear, grief, sadness, or something else, but in each case, the sticking point is a belief that you won't be able to handle feeling that way.

This might be another example of "catastrophizing"—imagining that the worst will happen and that it will be completely intolerable. Examine the evidence: Have you felt bad before? Undoubtedly. Was there ever a time that you felt bad, but you didn't have a complete meltdown and you were able to go on with life? Probably so. Is this situation similar? If so, you probably have the capacity to cope with what you are feeling, and doing so will actually make you stronger.

Another common thinking error is "discounting the positive." This is focusing exclusively on the negative elements of the situation, without acknowledging the positive. For example, you may have found yourself dwelling on how unpleasant the task of sorting and organizing was, worrying about mistakes you might make, or grieving for the loss of things you have discarded, without giving yourself credit for the progress you have made. Take a moment and pat yourself on the back. By working on your hoarding problem, even though aspects of it might be uncomfortable, you are making progress. Bit by bit, you will notice the situation improving, and the uncomfortable feelings will become less frequent and less intense.

✏️ Downward Arrow

Think about the worst thing that can happen if unpleasant feelings show up. The form below will help.

Item:_____

As you think about sorting, organizing, and discarding, what kind of unpleasant feelings do you anticipate?

_____

_____

If you did feel that way, what would be the worst thing that could happen?

_____

_____

If that did happen, what's so bad about that?

_____

_____

How long do you think it would take you to recover?

_____

_____

Testing It Out

Now that you've identified the worst thing that would happen if you experienced unpleasant feelings, try imagining that outcome vividly—if you imagine having a complete mental breakdown, for example, running amok, screaming, and tearing your hair out. On a scale of 0 to 10, how vivid and scary does that image seem? Now think about it some more, in great detail. Keep thinking about it for 10 straight minutes, without stopping. Really imagine it happening. Using the same 0-to-10 scale, how vivid and scary does the image seem now? Most of the time, when we allow ourselves to imagine the worst and stick with that image for a while, it starts to seem less realistic and perhaps even a bit silly.

Bad Guy #3: Going for the Short-Term Payoff

The path of least resistance can be awfully tempting. We all have a natural tendency to do what feels best at the moment instead of what we know is good for us. When you feel uncomfortable or upset about getting rid of something you realize you don't need to keep, it's easier to feel better right now by saving it. When we see a "treasure" or a great bargain, we often can't help but imagine the thrill of acquiring it. These are short-term payoffs that make us feel better momentarily. Unfortunately, the long-term consequences are more clutter and frustration. Overcoming this tendency is an important part of making a sustained change.

Thinking It Through

Sometimes we engage in "emotional reasoning": believing that something is true because of how it feels. Some examples of emotional reasoning include:

"It feels uncomfortable to put this out of sight, so I'll just leave it here."

"It bothers me to leave this without buying it, so I must need it."

"If I feel uncomfortable about throwing this away, this means I should keep it."

"It just seems like there must be something important in this paper. I better keep it."

Your best weapon against emotional reasoning is to stop, identify the error, and examine the evidence. How reliable are your gut feelings? Have they always been accurate? Have you ever felt one way about something, and then it turned out another way?

Keeping Your Eyes on the Prize

When short-term payoffs beckon, it's important to step back and remember what it is you are trying to accomplish—look at the forest, not just the trees. In Chapter 7, you identified some important reasons for beating hoarding. These are the things that are really important, much more so than the object in your hand or on the store shelf. Remember too that you are making progress, and give yourself credit for that. It's also critical that you make working on hoarding as rewarding as possible. In Chapter 9, you established a reward system, in which you would give yourself a specific reward—say, a favorite activity—if and only if you spent the necessary amount of time working on hoarding. Have you stuck with that plan? If not, it's time to implement it. Make sure you give yourself a small reward every time you work on hoarding for the specified amount of time. But give yourself that reward ONLY if you do the work.

Your Practice Muscle

The stronger your Practice Muscle, the less likely you will be to go for the short-term payoff. You will be surprised how much easier it is to keep your goals in mind when your Practice Muscle Strength is above 30.

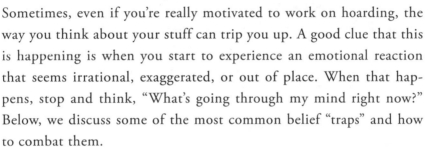

12

Here Come the Bad Guys
Part 2. Taking on Your Brain

Bad Guy #4: Letting Unhelpful Beliefs About Your Stuff Get in Your Way

Sometimes, even if you're really motivated to work on hoarding, the way you think about your stuff can trip you up. A good clue that this is happening is when you start to experience an emotional reaction that seems irrational, exaggerated, or out of place. When that happens, stop and think, "What's going through my mind right now?" Below, we discuss some of the most common belief "traps" and how to combat them.

Beliefs About Usefulness

When Bill started sorting and organizing, he found that he was putting almost everything in the "keep" pile. He wasn't going to make much progress that way! We asked him to hold something—an old clock-radio—in his hands, and talk about what he was thinking. He said, "I could probably fix this up and use it; it would be a shame to waste it."

Thinking It Through

Go back to the questions you generated when you were thinking through items in Chapter 10. This might prompt you to come up with some really good questions that apply to this specific item and your specific circumstances, but here are some to stimulate your thinking:

- How many do I already have, and is that enough?
- Do I have enough time to actually use, review, or read it?
- Have I used this in the past year?
- Do I have a specific plan to use this item within a reasonable timeframe?
- Does this fit with my own values and needs?
- How does this compare with the things I value highly?
- Does this seem important just because I'm looking at it now?
- Is it current?
- Is it of good quality, accurate, and/or reliable?
- Is it easy to understand?
- Would I buy it again if I didn't already own it?
- Do I really need it?
- Could I get it again if I found I really needed it?
- Do I have enough space for this?
- Will not having this help me solve my hoarding problem?

Advantages/Disadvantages

Think about the advantages and disadvantages of saving this item, as well as the advantages and disadvantages of letting it go. Here's a worksheet for you to list all of the things you think of. Write your advantages and disadvantages on the sheet, and see if that helps tip the scale in favor of letting go.

➥❖ Advantages/Disadvantages Worksheet

Specify the item(s) under consideration:

_____

_____

Advantages (Benefits) of keeping/ acquiring:	Disadvantages (Costs) of keeping/ acquiring:
_____	_____
_____	_____

_____   _____

_____   _____

_____   _____

_____   _____

_____   _____

_____   _____

_____   _____

We'd also like you to think about whether you really *need* this item or whether you just *want* it. To *need* something means that you absolutely must have it and would have a very hard time doing without it. *Wanting* something, on the other hand, means that you would like to keep it, and perhaps keeping it would make you feel better than letting it go, but you would be OK without it. Below, rate the extent to which you *need* and *want* the item.

Item being considered: _____

Rate your need for the item on the scale below:

Need Scale

0   1   2   3   4   5   6   7   8   9   10

No need   Required to
                                             survive

Rate how much you want or desire the item on this scale:

Want Scale

0   1   2   3   4   5   6   7   8   9   10

Don't want   Desperate for

Now, let's consider the value of the item more carefully.

To evaluate your true NEED for it, consider whether you need it for survival, safety, health, work, financial affairs, and/or recreation using the following questions:

- Would you die without it?
- Would your safety be impaired without it?
- Would your health be jeopardized without it?
- Is this critical to your work or employment?
- Is this needed to keep your financial records in order (e.g., tax or insurance records)?

Re-rate your need for the item below:

Need Scale

0	1	2	3	4	5	6	7	8	9	10

No need   Required to survive

Take a moment and think about how you feel about this item now. Are you ready to try letting go of it? If so, congratulations—you've changed your thinking pattern so it no longer controls you. Let go of the item by putting it in its designated place (e.g., the garbage can, recycle bin, or a box of things to donate or sell).

Testing It Out

If you still are having difficulty letting go of the item, let's try a testing-it-out exercise to see whether your need for this item is as pronounced as your brain is telling you it is. Start by making a specific prediction below.

What is the item you identified? _____

What bad outcome would happen if you let go of the item?

_____

How difficult would it be for you to recover if that bad thing happened? _____ (0–10)

Now let's try something. We'd like you to experiment with living without the item. Don't worry, no one's going to make you throw it away; for now, we just want you to see whether this prediction comes true. Take the item and put it somewhere you can't get to it. You might put it in the trunk of your car, or give it to a friend or family member for a while. The idea is to make it *as if* you don't have it. Let it stay there for a week, then come back to this section. Did the bad outcome you predicted actually occur? Most likely, nothing bad happened and you didn't miss the item after a while. That's an important sign that you can live without it. Even if there was a bad outcome from doing without the item, does it still seem as difficult to recover as you had predicted?

Perfectionism and Fear of Making Mistakes

Perhaps you have found that when considering what to do with an item, you start worrying about making a mistake or getting the decision wrong. As Helen was sorting, she found herself paralyzed by her fears, saying to herself, "What if I accidentally throw away something important? What if I mess up? The results would be disastrous!"

Give yourself permission to make mistakes.

Alternatively, you might have found yourself making partial, but not complete, progress in this program. It's easy to label this a "failure" and get down on yourself. This, in turn, leads to feelings of helplessness and increases your risk of giving up.

Thinking It Through

Often, perfectionism stems from common mistakes in thinking. One of these, called "all-or-nothing thinking," means thinking in terms of black and white without considering shades of gray (moderation). Some examples of all-or-nothing thinking are:

"If I can't figure out the perfect place to put this, I should just leave it here."

"I can't get rid of this until I read and remember everything in this newspaper."

"Now I will forget everything I know about this subject."

"If I don't make visible progress every day, I'm failing."

If you catch yourself thinking all-or-nothing thoughts, stop and ask yourself: Is that really true? Do I really have to put this in the perfect place? Do I really have to remember everything about it? Am I really failing at this? What is the evidence to support that statement?

Another common error in thinking is called "catastrophizing," or making mountains out of molehills. We catastrophize when we tell ourselves that the consequences of making a mistake will be terrible, awful, horrible, and so forth. Here are some examples of catastrophic thinking:

"If I put this away and can't remember where I put it, it will be awful."

"If I don't have this information when I need it, that's when I'll find out it could have saved my husband's life."

"I'll fall apart if I don't have this."

"If I throw it away, I'll go crazy thinking about it."

"I'll never forgive myself."

Again, if you catch yourself doing this, it's time for a reality check. Would it really be awful? Would you never be able to recover if you made a mistake? Would the world come to an end?

There's an old saying: You can't make an omelet without breaking some eggs. Mistakes happen. If you have a lot of clutter to go through, it's inevitable that at some point you will discard something that has potential value, put something in the wrong place, store something improperly, or mess up in some other way. Give yourself permission to make mistakes. Remember, your top priority here is to beat hoarding and reduce the clutter in your home (if it's not, go back to page 35). If some mistakes occur along the way, it won't be the end of the world.

Downward Arrow

This is a great opportunity to use the downward arrow to help clarify and challenge your thinking. Below you'll find a worksheet to help you; write your answers in the spaces provided.

Item: _____

In thinking about letting go of (discarding, recycling, selling, giving away) this item, what kind of mistake are you worried about making?

_____

_____

_____

If you did make a mistake, why would it be so upsetting? (What would it mean to you? Why would that be so bad?)

_____

_____

If that were true, what's so bad about that?

_____

_____

What's the worst part about that?

_____

_____

What does that mean about *you*?

_____

_____

Testing It Out

Now let's try something really unusual—a testing-it-out exercise about making mistakes. For this exercise, we'd like you to make a small mistake *on purpose*. That's right; we actually want you to try to mess up a little. For example, you might consider throwing away something you normally would want to hang on to (as long as the results wouldn't be truly disastrous to you), like a bank statement. Start by deciding what kind of mistake you'll make, and then write a specific prediction below.

What kind of mistake do you plan to make? _____

What do you fear will happen when you make that mistake?

_____

How difficult would it be for you to recover if that bad thing happened? _____ (0–10)

Now, take a very brave step and *make that mistake.* See what happens. Does the bad outcome actually occur? Was it as hard to recover as you thought it would be?

Beliefs About Responsibility

Do you feel guilty when you try to get rid of things or not acquire things, as if you are being irresponsible or wasteful? Bill felt guilty when he tried to get rid of things he might be able to fix, even when the likelihood that he would or even could fix it was zero. Even the idea of throwing it out made him feel like a wasteful and bad person. Even for those things that he thought he could part with, he felt compelled to make sure that they went to a "good home." Similarly, Helen collected things for other people, things she thought they might like or want. If she saw something like this, she felt guilty if she didn't buy it. Many of these items collected dust in her house because her friends didn't want them. We'll tackle responsibility beliefs in a way similar to how we addressed perfectionism—with a downward arrow and testing it out.

Downward Arrow

Write down your thoughts about responsibility below.

●◆ Downward Arrow Form

Item: _____

In thinking about letting go of (discarding, recycling, selling, giving away) this item, in what way do you fear you will act irresponsibly?

_____

_____

_____

If you did act irresponsibly, why would it be so upsetting? (What would it mean to you? Why would that be so bad?)

_____

_____

If that were true, what's so bad about that?

_____

_____

What's the worst part about that?

_____

_____

What does that mean about *you*?

_____

_____

Testing It Out

Now let's try a testing-it-out exercise about acting irresponsibly. For this exercise, we'd like you to act irresponsibly, in some small way, *on purpose*. For example, you might throw something away that is fixable or still useful, or try moving something from the recycle bin to the garbage can, even though it's recyclable. The idea is to do something that challenges your assumptions about responsibility. We are not advocating a wasteful lifestyle, but we do want you to develop enough control over your beliefs about responsibility that you can live responsibly without compromising your living conditions. You can do this by experimenting with mildly irresponsible acts. Start by deciding how you will act irresponsibly, and then write a specific prediction below.

What kind of irresponsible action do you plan to take? _____

_____

What do you fear will happen when you take that irresponsible action?

_____

How difficult would it be for you to recover if that bad thing happened? _____ (0–10)

Now, go ahead and actually do it. See what happens. Does the bad outcome actually occur? Was it as hard to recover as you thought it would be?

Attachments to Possessions

Sometimes, people hang on to something because they feel emotionally attached to it. Even though the item doesn't have much practical use, our sense of attachment can be a powerful motivator to hang on to it. The problem is that many people who hoard feel a sense of attachment not to just one or two items, but rather to so many items that they don't feel able to reduce the clutter in their homes.

Thinking It Through

Start by deciding just how attached you feel to the object. Below is a scale to rate your level of attachment; rate your feelings as they are right now.

Attachment Scale

0	1	2	3	4	5	6	7	8	9	10
Not at all attached									Completely attached	

Did you give yourself a high score? If so, try asking yourself some challenging questions. Here are some questions we use, but perhaps you can think of others that are more effective for you—that's why we included some blank spaces at the bottom.

- How much do you actually look at or enjoy this object?
- Are you keeping it for sentimental reasons? If so, does it truly make you happy to have it?

- Are you keeping it as a way of remembering good times or a special person? If so, is keeping it the best way to remember? If that person could see your home, what would he/she encourage you to do?
- Do you keep this for emotional comfort or to make you feel less vulnerable? If so, does it really protect you?
- Is this object really a friend or companion? Does it have thoughts and feelings, or is it just a thing?
- _____
- _____

Now that you've asked yourself some tough questions, try rating your level of attachment again, using the scale above. Did your attachment level decrease to the point where you are now ready to try letting go of the item? If not, it's time to try...

Testing It Out

Let's try an exercise to see if you can reduce your feelings of attachment. For this exercise, we'll ask you to try distancing yourself by putting the object somewhere you can't get to it, like in the trunk of your car or at a friend's or family member's home. Start by writing a specific prediction below.

Where will you put the item? _____

How do you imagine you will feel when you do that?
_____

How strong do you think that feeling will be?
_____ (0–10)

How difficult would it be for you to recover if you felt that way?
_____ (0–10)

Let the object stay there for a week, without looking at it. Then come back to this section.

Did things turn out the way you predicted? _____

How did you actually feel without the item? _____

How strong was the feeling in reality? _____ (0–10)

How difficult was it for you to recover from bad feelings?
_____ (0–10)

Beliefs About Objects as a Source of Identity

You may recall that Bill derived a strong sense of identity from his possessions. As he looked around his home, he saw countless opportunities: things he could fix, things he could sell, and so on. Much of the pleasure Bill got from his possessions was how they made him feel about himself, and the ideas he generated about the person he wanted to be. When Bill's family members came to his home, however, they saw things differently. Instead of appreciating the numerous opportunities and the potential for Bill to become an entrepreneur and handyman, they saw clutter. They noticed that Bill held on to his possessions but never actually got around to fixing them or selling them. He had, in a sense, become trapped by his identity-related beliefs.

Thinking It Through

If you start noticing yourself reacting to your possessions with identity-related beliefs, try asking yourself some straightforward questions. What kind of identity do you derive from your possessions?

- *My possessions make me feel like a craftsperson or artist.* Many people save items because they think they can use them for art projects or crafts. Think about how much art or crafts you have produced in the past year—not what you planned to produce or ideas that you generated, but what you actually produced. Are the materials you save proportional to the amount you actually produce?
- *My possessions make me feel like a handyperson.* Some people save worn or broken things with the idea that they will fix them later. How many of these things do you currently have in your home? How many have you actually fixed or renovated in the past year? How many can you realistically expect to fix or renovate this year?

- *My possessions make me feel like a businessperson or entrepreneur.* Still others keep things in the hopes of selling them or starting a business with them. If you are holding on to things like this, what steps have you taken so far to actually sell them or start that business? Is it reasonable to conclude that you will be able to do so in the near future?
- *My possessions make me feel like a good family member or friend.* Finally, some people save things they plan to give to their loved ones. How many potential gifts are in your home? How long have they been there? How many gifts have you actually given in the past year?

You may notice a common theme in these questions: is the amount you *have* proportional to the amount you *do*? The point we'd like to make here is that for most people, identity comes from what we do. A craftsperson is someone who produces crafts. A handyperson is someone who fixes things. A businessperson is someone who starts a business and earns income. A good family member or friend is someone who does good things for others. For many people with hoarding, however, their possessions give them a false sense of identity: by accumulating and hanging on to items, they feel *as if* they have that identity, even though they really don't. No amount of art supplies can make you an artist. No amount of ungiven gifts can make you generous. True, some stuff is necessary for certain activities that, in turn, lead to an identity. However, many people who hoard get stuck on the initial step—acquiring the stuff—and don't move on to the more important action parts of the process.

Since your possessions can't define your identity, it will be important to *redefine your identity without clutter.* What is the identity you really want? Who do you want to be? What do you want your life to be about? These are big questions, with no simple answers, but it's important to think about them nevertheless—they are about what you value most in life. If you decide you want to be a craftsperson, entrepreneur, good family member, and so forth, is there a way to achieve that identity without keeping a large volume of clutter in your home? If you want to be an artist, how could you achieve that without clutter? Perhaps you could let go of many of your art supplies, saving only those that are critical to the art you want to produce, and then actually spend your time making art. If you want to be a generous person, perhaps this would be a good time to donate many of your possessions to a charitable organization or give them as gifts to friends or family.

Underestimating Memory

Part of Helen's problem was the fact that she consistently underestimated the strength of her memory. Because she worried so intensely that she would forget something important, her solution was to leave things in sight so that she would remember them. Of course, the problem with this strategy was that eventually the clutter piled up to the point that she couldn't find things she needed. Thus, her "memory-enhancing" strategy was actually memory-*damaging*.

Testing It Out

Let's try an exercise to see whether your memory is good enough to find the things that you need, even when you've put them out of sight. Pick five things you might forget and put them somewhere out of sight, to see if you forget them. Choose things that are relatively small, so that you can easily move them. Once you have identified the objects, put them somewhere that makes logical sense. In other words, if you are holding a letter, it doesn't make much sense to store it in the bathroom or garage; rather, it should be stored in a desk drawer or, better yet, a correspondence file that you have created. Write down the five items and where you put them (just in case).

Item	Where I put it
1. _____	_____
2. _____	_____
3. _____	_____
4. _____	_____
5. _____	_____

Now wait 24 hours, and see if you can find the items. Did you find all five of them? If so, you may have underestimated your memory, and there is no need for you to keep things in sight. If you were unable to find all five of them, however, you might in fact have some problems with memory and will need to make use of some of the memory-helping strategies described below.

Developing the Right Skills

If you do find it difficult to remember where items are stored, it might be because you are asking too much of your memory. Developing effective and efficient organizational strategies will help you rely less on your memory and more on an external structure. In Chapter 9, you listed categories of items that you wanted to save, and the location of each category. Go back and look at that list, and use it as a guide for sorting. We often find that people overtax their memories, particularly when it comes to paper items such as bills, checks, correspondence, and so on. Therefore, it will be helpful to review the strategies for organizing paper items in Chapter 9. If you haven't done so already, we recommend you identify a specific place to store paper items. A file cabinet is perfect, but if you don't have one or can't afford one, a large plastic container or cardboard box will work; just make sure it is the right size to store your papers. You will need a good supply of file folders, such as the manila kind, and a pen to label the files. Label the files as directed in Chapter 9, and then place them in alphabetical order in the storage container. As you sort papers and decide to keep them, place them in the appropriate file folder. This way, you won't have to rely on your memory as much. Instead of having to remember where every little thing is (e.g., where you keep your stamps, your coupons, your medical information, etc.), you need only remember that paper items go in the storage container. Instead of having to remember 20 or 30 different things, you now have to remember only one.

Beliefs About Control

Sometimes, people hang onto things not because they necessarily intend to use them or feel attached to them, but rather because they feel it's their right to do so. For example, Bill told us that the more his adult daughter complained about the clutter and asked him to get rid of it, the more he tended to hold on to it. He complained, "No one has the right to tell me what to do with my stuff." And he was right: it was his stuff, and he certainly had the right to do with it as he pleased. But, as you might have guessed, there was a downside to this: the more he dug in his heels, the more stuck he became.

Thinking It Through

Do you find that your control-related beliefs make it hard for you to let go of things? Does hanging on to things give you a sense of control? If so, perhaps it would help to ask yourself some challenging questions:

- Are you really in control, or are your possessions controlling you?
- Does letting go of possessions really mean that you will lose control? What would happen then?
- Are you trying to make sure that someone else doesn't "win"? Are you really "winning" by hanging on to these things?

Bad Guy #5: Overthinking or Confusing Yourself

As we discussed in Chapter 4, overthinking or confusing yourself can present in three different ways: over-creativity, burdensome rules for discarding, and too many categories. In this section, we'll discuss how to beat each of these problems.

Bill's over-creativity—his tendency to think of more and more ways to use an object—got the better of him. When he held an object in his hands, he couldn't help but think of all of the wonderful opportunities it represented. Because he was a very creative person, he could easily think of lots of ways to use the object. A piece of rope wasn't just a piece of rope: in his mind, it was a clothesline, a way to keep his car trunk closed when he went out acquiring, a way to secure a tarp over his bicycle, an emergency escape in case of fire, and on and on it went. Technically, Bill was right: a rope *could* be used for all those things. But if we take a step back and look at the situation clearly, we can see that Bill's over-creativity was working against him, not for him. He thought of many uses for objects and never got around to actually letting go of them. It bears mentioning as well that most of the uses he thought of existed only in his mind, not in his actions. Although he could think of lots of ways to use the rope, he didn't actually use the rope in those ways; rather, the rope remained unused on top of a pile of clutter.

Developing the Right Skills

One way to reduce over-creativity is to learn to speed up the decision-making process. Get a kitchen timer that has an audible alarm. Start by figuring out approximately how long it takes you to make a decision about whether to keep or let go of an object. To accomplish this, you'll need to try it a few times. Come up with a rough estimate of your average decision-making time. Now, set the kitchen timer for approximately half that time. For example, if you find that it takes you an average of 10 minutes to make a decision about an object, set the timer for 5 minutes. Try to have the decision-making process finished by the time the alarm goes off. It may take you a few tries, but eventually you will probably find that, more often than not, you can make your decision in that amount of time. When you have accomplished that goal, divide the time in half again. For example, this time try setting the alarm for 2.5 minutes instead of 5. Keep practicing until you are able to make your decisions in that amount of time. An ideal goal would be for you eventually to be able to make your decisions in 1 minute or less per item. That may seem awfully fast, but we have found that with practice, you can do it.

Thinking It Through

If you catch yourself thinking of new, creative ways to use the objects you pick up during sorting and discarding, stop and ask yourself: Am I really and truly going to use the object in this way, or is my creativity just getting the better of me? Does this object really represent a wonderful opportunity, or is it just clutter taking up space in my home?

Helen's overthinking showed itself in the excessively difficult and burdensome rules she had set forth for letting go of things. When she tried to sort and discard newspapers, she thought carefully about doing it just right. She wanted the bundle of newspapers to be easy to handle, to ensure that the bundles would not come apart while being transported, and to make sure that the recycling crew did not think badly of her because she left sloppy bundles of newspapers at the curbside. As a result, she had to create newspaper bundles of a certain size, tied carefully with just the right kind of string, without any wrinkles, with the glossy advertising inserts removed. The problem was that these "rules" were so exacting that they became a burden. Instead of being a relatively easy and straightforward process, sorting and discarding newspapers became a major ordeal. Eventually, Helen just gave up.

Another common error of thinking in cases like this is making "should" statements to yourself. "Should" statements occur when we tell ourselves how things *should* be, how they *must* be, or how they *ought* to be. Stop and ask yourself some challenging questions:

- Is this really a rule? Where is it written that I have to do things exactly this way?
- Does everyone follow these "rules"? What happens when they don't?

Downward Arrow

Write down your thoughts about "rules" for discarding below.

◗◆ Downward Arrow Form

Item: _____

In thinking about letting go of (discarding, recycling, selling, giving away) this item, what rule(s) do you believe you have to follow?

If you violated that rule, what would be the worst thing that could happen?

_____

If that did happen, what's so bad about that?

_____

_____

What's the worst part about that?

_____

_____

What does that mean about *you*?

_____

_____

Testing It Out

A great way to beat "should" statements is to experiment with breaking the rules. So for this exercise, we'd like you to identify a "rule" that you have set for yourself in your sorting and discarding—for example, "I should check if my coworker wants the magazine before I get rid of it." Then, we want you to break the rule and see what happens. Start by writing a specific prediction below.

What rule will you break? _____

What do you think will happen as a result of breaking that rule?

_____

If that bad outcome did occur, how bad would it be?
_____ (0–10)

Now, break the rule. For example, for the rule about the magazine above, just put the magazine in the garbage can without consulting your coworker first.

What actually happened when you broke the rule?

_____

How bad was the outcome in reality? _____ (0–10)

Way back in Chapter 2, we described a research study we had conducted in which we seated people at a table covered with stuff and then asked them to sort the stuff into categories. We found that people who hoard made a lot more categories than did people who don't hoard. This only occurred, however, when the stuff on the table actually belonged to the person. When it didn't belong to them, people with and without hoarding problems came up with the same number of categories. It wasn't that people who hoard were bad at categorizing; they were just bad at categorizing *their possessions*. What does this mean in real life? We need only watch Helen try to sort her possessions to see how this plays out. As she tried to sort a pile of mail on her kitchen counter, she created a large number of piles: credit card offers with 0 percent financing, credit card offers with low rates but not 0 percent, credit card offers with high rates, magazine subscription offers, charity solicitations, and so on. Although this level of precision satisfied some of her perfectionistic tendencies, it created two major problems for her. First, it was incredibly time-consuming. The more categories she created, the more she had to think about each item, and the longer the process took, until she just stopped doing it. Second, once she had created all these piles, she didn't know what to do with them. Her precise and detailed sorting style turned into a waste of her time and energy.

Developing the Right Skills

To make your sorting and organizing more efficient, you must learn to reduce the number of categories you use. In Chapter 9, you wrote a list of categories for your possessions. Go back and take a look at that list, and try to stick to it as you sort. Think about whether any of your categories can be combined—for example, by combining the categories "dress shoes" and "sneakers," Helen was able to sort her shoes more efficiently, having one less thing to have to think about.

✳ Taking on the Bad Guys

By now you have a pretty good idea of which bad guys keep you from solving your hoarding problem. They can be difficult to detect because everyone thinks this way, at least some of the time. Because you are prone to these ways of thinking, it is important to decide what are good reasons to save things and what are bad reasons (bad guys). Whenever the bad guys occur, challenge them. Gradually, you will train yourself to react differently and gain control over your hoarding problem.

13

Maintaining Your Success

Once you have had success in decluttering or controlling your hoarding, you must now face the important task of maintaining what you have accomplished. The first step is to make an honest appraisal of what you have accomplished in your efforts to control this problem.

❋ Checking the Photographs

At the beginning of this program, we asked you to take some photographs of your home. Hopefully you stored them electronically so they didn't add to the clutter. It's time to go take another look at them. Look carefully at each picture, then look at the condition of those same spaces now. Try to take a good honest look: what's better? What's not better? It's important to be balanced here—if parts of your home look better now than they did at the beginning, then give yourself a big pat on the back and congratulate yourself on your success! And if parts of your home don't look better, just recognize that these areas are where you're going to need to do some more work.

After you've had a chance to look at your photos, fill out the measures here. They may look familiar to you—you completed the same forms in Chapter 3. Without peeking at Chapter 3, complete them based on how things are for you right now.

For each question below, circle the number that corresponds most closely to your experience DURING THE PAST WEEK.

1. Because of the clutter or number of possessions, how difficult is it for you to use the rooms in your home?

0	1	2	3	4	5	6	7	8
Not at all difficult		Mildly difficult		Moderately difficult		Severely difficult		Extremely difficult

2. To what extent do you have difficulty discarding (or recycling, selling, giving away) ordinary things that other people would get rid of?

0	1	2	3	4	5	6	7	8
No difficulty		Mild difficulty		Moderate difficulty		Severe difficulty		Extreme difficulty

3. To what extent do you currently have a problem with collecting free things or buying more things than you need or can use or can afford?

0	1	2	3	4	5	6	7	8
No problem		Mild problem		Moderate problem		Severe problem		Extreme problem

4. To what extent do you experience emotional distress because of clutter, difficulty discarding, or problems with buying or acquiring things?

0	1	2	3	4	5	6	7	8
None		Mild		Moderate		Severe		Extreme

5. To what extent do you experience impairment in your life (daily routine, job/school, social activities, family activities, financial difficulties) because of clutter, difficulty discarding, or problems with buying or acquiring things?

0	1	2	3	4	5	6	7	8
None		Mild		Moderate		Severe		Extreme

The next test will help you identify the degree to which the features of hoarding are affecting the safety and quality of your life.

Safety is a concern when hoarding is severe. Answer these questions to determine whether there are safety issues you need to address.

Type of problem	None	Somewhat/ A little	Moderate	Substantial	Severe
1. Is there any structural damage to the floors, walls, roof, or other parts of your home?	1	2	3	4	5
2. Does any part of your house pose a fire hazard (e.g., stove covered with paper, flammable objects near the furnace, etc.)?	1	2	3	4	5
3. Are parts of your house unsanitary (bathrooms unclean, strong odor)?	1	2	3	4	5
4. Would medical emergency personnel have difficulty moving equipment through your home?	1	2	3	4	5
5. Are any exits from your home blocked?	1	2	3	4	5
6. Is it unsafe to move up or down the stairs or along other walkways?	1	2	3	4	5
7. Is there clutter outside your house (porch, yard, alleyway, common areas if apartment or condo)?	1	2	3	4	5

Add your scores for items 1–7. _____

This is your *Safety* score.

Your scores can be classified as:

7-13	Minimal
14-20	Mild
21-27	Moderate
28-30	Severe
31-35	Very severe

If you scored 21 or higher (moderate or worse), you may be living in an unsafe home. If you scored 3 or higher on any one question, this should be a high-priority item to be addressed right away.

●◖◗ Are Your Daily Activities Impaired by Hoarding?

Sometimes clutter in the home can prevent you from doing ordinary activities. For each of the following activities, please circle the number that best represents the degree of difficulty you experience in doing this activity because of the clutter or hoarding problem. If you have difficulty with the activity for other reasons (for example, unable to bend or move quickly due to physical problems), do not include this in your rating. Instead, rate only how much difficulty you have due to hoarding. If the activity is not relevant to your situation (for example, you don't have laundry facilities or animals), check the Not Applicable (NA) box.

Activities affected by clutter or hoarding problem	Can do it easily	Can do it with a little difficulty	Can do it with moderate difficulty	Can do it with great difficulty	Unable to do	NA
1. Prepare food	1	2	3	4	5	NA
2. Use refrigerator	1	2	3	4	5	NA
3. Use stove	1	2	3	4	5	NA
4. Use kitchen sink	1	2	3	4	5	NA
5. Eat at table	1	2	3	4	5	NA
6. Move around inside the house	1	2	3	4	5	NA
7. Exit home quickly	1	2	3	4	5	NA
8. Use toilet	1	2	3	4	5	NA
9. Use bath/shower	1	2	3	4	5	NA
10. Use bathroom sink	1	2	3	4	5	NA
11. Answer door quickly	1	2	3	4	5	NA
12. Sit in sofa/chair	1	2	3	4	5	NA
13. Sleep in bed	1	2	3	4	5	NA
14. Do laundry	1	2	3	4	5	NA
15. Find important things (such as bills, tax forms, etc.)	1	2	3	4	5	NA

These questions assess the extent to which clutter causes problems in daily functioning at home.

Step 1: Add your scores for items 1–15, excluding items with NA (not applicable) ratings. _____

Step 2: Indicate the number of questions in items 1–15 that have a numeric score (i.e., not an NA rating) _____

Step 3: Divide the first number by the second number.

_____

For example, if your total score for items 1–15 was 45, and you gave numeric ratings for 14 items (meaning you made 2 NA ratings), your score is 45 ÷ 14 = 3.21. This is your *Activities of Daily Living* score.

Your scores can be classified as:

1.0–1.4   Minimal
1.5–2.0   Mild
2.1–3.0   Moderate
3.1–4.0   Severe
4.1–5.0   Very severe

If you scored 2.5 or higher (moderate or worse), the clutter has caused substantial difficulties in your ability to function in your home.

🔑 Does Hoarding Affect the Sanitary Condition of Your Home?

Home Environment Index

Clutter and hoarding problems can sometimes lead to sanitation problems. Please circle the answer that best fits the current situation in the home.

To what extent are the following situations present in the home?

1. Fire hazard

    0 = No fire hazard
    1 = Some risk of fire (for example, lots of flammable material)
    2 = Moderate risk of fire (for example, flammable materials near heat source)
    3 = High risk of fire (for example, flammable materials near heat source, electrical hazards, etc.)

2. Moldy or rotten food

    0 = None
    1 = A few pieces of moldy or rotten food in kitchen
    2 = Some moldy or rotten food throughout kitchen
    3 = Large quantity of moldy or rotten food in kitchen and elsewhere

3. Dirty or clogged sink

    0 = Sink empty and clean
    1 = A few dirty dishes with water in sink
    2 = Sink full of water, possibly clogged
    3 = Sink clogged with evidence that it has overflowed onto counters, etc.

4. Standing water (in sink, tub, other container, basement, etc.)

    0 = No standing water
    1 = Some water in sink/tub
    2 = Water in several places, especially if dirty
    3 = Water in numerous places, especially if dirty

5. Human/animal waste/vomit

    0 = No human waste, animal waste, or vomit visible
    1 = Small amojunt of human or animal waste (e.g., unflushed toilet, on bathroom or other floor)
    2 = Moderate animal or human waste or vomit visible in more than one room
    3 = Animal or human waste or vomit on floors or other surfaces

6. Mildew or mold

    0 = No mildew or mold detectable
    1 = Small amount of mildew or mold in limited amounts and expected places (for example, on edge of shower curtain or refrigerator seal)
    2 = Considerable, noticeable mildew or mold
    3 = Widespread mildew or mold on most surfaces

7. Dirty food containers

    0 = All dishes washed and put away
    1 = A few unwashed dishes
    2 = Many unwashed dishes
    3 = Almost all dishes are unwashed

8. Dirty surfaces (floors, walls, furniture, etc.)

    0 = Surfaces completely clean
    1 = A few spills, some dirt or grime

2 = More than a few spills, may be a thin covering of dirt or grime in living areas

3 = No surface is clean; dirt or grime covers everything

9. Piles of dirty or contaminated objects (bathroom tissue, hair, toilet paper, sanitary products, etc.)

0 = No dirty or contaminated objects on floors, surfaces, etc.

1 = Some dirty or contaminated objects present around trash cans or toilets

2 = Many dirty or contaminated objects fill bathroom or area around trash cans

3 = Dirty or contaminated objects cover the floors and surfaces in most rooms

10. Insects

0 = No insects are visible

1 = A few insects visible; cobwebs and/or insect droppings present

2 = Many insects and droppings are visible; cobwebs in corners

3 = Swarms of insects; high volume of droppings; many cobwebs on household items

11. Dirty clothes

0 = Dirty clothes placed in hamper; none are lying around

1 = Hamper is full; a few dirty clothes lying around

2 = Hamper is overflowing; many dirty clothes lying around

3 = Clothes cover the floor and many other surfaces (bed, chairs, etc.)

12. Dirty bed sheets/linens

0 = Bed coverings very clean

1 = Bed coverings relatively clean

2 = Bed coverings dirty and in need of washing

3 = Bed coverings very dirty and soiled

13. Odor of house

0 = No odor

1 = Slight odor

2 = Moderate odor; may be strong in some parts of house

3 = Strong odor throughout house

During the last month, how often did you (or someone in your home) do each of the following activities?

14. Do the dishes

0 = Daily or every 2 days; 15 to 30 times per month

1 = 1 or 2 times a week; 4 to 10 times per month

2 = Every other week; 2 or 3 times per month

3 = Rarely; 0 times per month

15. Clean the bathroom

0 = Daily or every 2 days; more than 10 times per month

1 = 1 or 2 times a week; 4 to 10 times per month

2 = Every other week; 2 or 3 times per month

3 = Never; 0 times per month

To score the HEI, sum the responses for all 15 items. The average score for a large Internet sample of people with hoarding was 12.7 (standard deviation = 6.9; range = 0–43). A score of 2 or above on any question warrants attention.

OK, you can peek now. Compare your current scores with the ones from Chapter 3. We hope that your scores show improvement. Give yourself a lot of credit for this. You've accomplished something that is not easy to do. The fact that you did it should be evidence to you that you have the power, control, and self-discipline to maintain what you've accomplished. Here are some suggestions that will help you do that.

✳ Establish a Schedule for Organizing

As you are no doubt aware, one reason hoarding gets out of control is that in the past you have avoided doing the sorting and letting go necessary to prevent it. If you set up a schedule for organizing and stick to it, you will maintain what you have accomplished. The condition of your Practice Muscle is important here. The more strictly you stick to your schedule, the easier it will get. Eventually it will become a habit that will feel just as natural to you as getting dressed in the morning. You will also see that making decisions about keeping, letting go, and organizing will get easier.

If you set up a schedule for organizing and stick to it, you will maintain what you have accomplished.

To be successful at sticking to a schedule, you will have to face a difficult fact: there will be many, many times when it seems to you that you are too tired, too upset, too busy, or too uninterested to stick to your schedule. If you give in to these feelings, your hoarding problems may come back. You must develop the strength to work *despite* being tired, upset, busy, or bored. Because you have had a problem with hoarding, keeping up with this schedule must be your highest priority.

It might help to think of yourself as a marathon runner. You have worked to get yourself into top-notch physical condition. However, if you stop exercising, your physical conditioning and stamina will decline. It is the same with organizing and decluttering. Sorting and letting go will become harder and harder unless you are doing it on a frequent and regular basis.

✳ Clutter Is a Magnet for Clutter

In the 1980s, social scientists James Wilson and George Kelling proposed what they called the "broken windows theory" of urban crime. They read about a famous study by psychologist Philip Zimbardo in which he left a car sitting in a nice neighborhood for 1 week. The car went untouched until Zimbardo smashed one of the car's windows. Within a day, the car had been completely stripped by thieves and vandals. Wilson and Kelling theorized that the presence of physical neglect or decay leads to a perception of disorder and chaos, leading people to behave accordingly. So, when people see a broken window, they figure it's OK to break more windows. Then, when lots of windows are broken, they figure that the area is rundown and therefore it's OK to do all kinds of rotten things. The broken windows theory has since been applied in police work and urban development, most visibly in New York City, where attention to smaller, "quality-of-life" problems (such as repairing signs of urban decay and stopping low-level crimes) seems to have reduced the occurrence of more serious crimes.

What does the broken windows theory have to do with you? Think about how your actions are influenced by clutter in your home. Now think about how your actions are influenced by cleanliness. When you have something in your hand—say, a piece of mail—it's very easy to put that item on top of a pile of clutter. You might think, "It's already such a mess; one more piece won't make much of a difference." On the other hand, you're less likely to put that item onto a clean surface. In that case, you might think, "I've worked so hard to make this area neat; I don't want to mess it up now," and you would be more likely to put the item where it belongs. This is another example of the broken windows principle—once clutter and disorganization start, we tend to add to it. *Clutter is a magnet for clutter.*

If you notice some clutter piling up, don't wait. Take care of it immediately.

This principle tells us that clear surfaces are one of your very best protections against the future buildup of clutter. If you notice some clutter piling up, don't wait. Take care of it immediately.

Make Rules for Organizing and Letting Go

In the course of this book we have suggested developing rules to help you make decisions about what to acquire or keep and where to put it. The task of maintaining your decluttered house will be much easier if you can set up and stick to a set of easy rules. For example, you might establish a rule that all junk mail (e.g., credit-card applications, advertisements, etc.) are put directly into the recycling bin as soon as you pick up your mail. Another might be that all bills go directly to a designated location (e.g., the desk) and are never set down anywhere else. Getting into the habit of handling your mail in this way is a simply strategy

Take a few minutes to set up five simple rules for yourself to maintain control over your hoarding.

for keeping down the clutter. Take a few minutes to set up five simple rules for yourself to maintain control over your hoarding. You may want to tape these rules to your refrigerator or somewhere easily visible until they become full-blown habits.

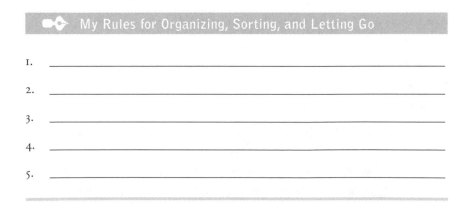

My Rules for Organizing, Sorting, and Letting Go

1. _____

2. _____

3. _____

4. _____

5. _____

✳ Bring Other People into Your Home

You may have noticed that as your hoarding problem grew worse, fewer and fewer people were coming into your home. Your social life may have suffered, but at the same time, your hoarding problem probably got worse because fewer people were coming to your home. Planning for visits by other people is a surefire way to improve your motivation to clean and organize. Whether or not we have a hoarding problem, visitors always get us to clean up.

Inviting visitors in also will get you into the habit of making your home a place to entertain. As you recall from the early chapters of this book, one of the major goals of this program is to be able to use your rooms in the ways they were intended. You have more than one chair in your living room so that more than one person can sit down, not so you have more objects to cover with your stuff. The more frequently you invite people into your home, the easier it will be for you to maintain what you have accomplished.

✳ Identify What Worked Best for You

Undoubtedly some of the exercises (the good guys) from earlier chapters worked better than others. You will be amazed at how powerful some of these techniques can be if you practice them enough. Take a moment and write in how each of these good guys helped you get control over your hoarding. Come back to this page from time to time to remind yourself of how you did it.

➤ How Good Guy #1: Keeping Your Eyes on the Prize Helped Me

_____

_____

_____

_____

☞ How Good Guy #2: Downward Arrow Helped Me

_____

_____

_____

_____

☞ How Good Guy #3: Thinking It Through Helped Me

_____

_____

_____

_____

☞ How Good Guy #4: Testing It Out Helped Me

_____

_____

_____

_____

☞ How Good Guy #5: Developing the Right Skills Helped Me

_____

_____

_____

_____

_____

_____

_____

_____

Challenging Your Thinking

If your hoarding problem is longstanding, you will probably still have some difficulties making decisions about certain things. Review the bad guys that have given you the most trouble. Spend a few minutes here to make notes about each of them and how you were able to overcome them. Make a plan for yourself to challenge these ways of thinking using the strategies you've learned in this book. Come back to this page from time to time to remind yourself of how these bad guys affected you.

How I Will Challenge Bad Guy #1: "It's just not my priority"

_____

_____

_____

_____

How I Will Challenge Bad Guy #2:
Avoidance and Excuse-Making

_____

_____

_____

_____

How I Will Challenge Bad Guy #3:
Going for the Short-Term Payoff

_____

_____

_____

_____

How I Will Challenge Bad Guy #4:
Letting Unhelpful Beliefs Get in My Way

_____

_____

_____

_____

How I Will Challenge Bad Guy #5:
Overthinking or Confusing Myself

_____

_____

_____

_____

❋ Cope With Setbacks

There may come a time when you find yourself losing the battle with your
possessions. As soon as you recognize that the clutter is building up again or
your credit-card bills are growing, go back and reread sections of this book
and work through the exercises again. Since you have succeeded once, you

can succeed again. A lot of people worry about "falling off the wagon" once they have gotten their hoarding under control. It happens, of course. But what's the best thing to do then? Lie down in the street while the wagon rolls away? Of course not. You get up, run alongside the wagon, and jump back on when you can. So it is with maintaining succes with this program. It's quite likely that you'll have lapses from time to time. You'll start buying unnecessary things, or the clutter will start building up. Recognize that this is normal, and it doesn't mean you've failed. It just means you have to do some more work to get back on track.

An important thing to remember is that stressful things happen to everyone, and we all must find a way to cope while at the same time keeping up with our ongoing responsibilities. When these events occur in your life, keep in mind that your organizing, sorting, and letting go are things that you need to maintain through thick and thin. Just like bathing, eating, or dressing, keeping your living space habitable is crucial to how well you can cope with stress. The more control you maintain over your hoarding, the better you will be able to cope with any stress.

> *The more control you maintain over your hoarding, the better you will be able to cope with any stress.*

✳ Use Available Resources

There are a number of Internet-based organizations to help with ongoing clutter management and support. Although this is by no means an exhaustive list, some of our clients have been pleased with the following Web sites:

International Obsessive Compulsive Disorder Foundation:
   www.ocfoundation.org/hoarding

   Children of Hoarders: www.childrenofhoarders.com

National Association of Professional Organizers: www.napo.net

Institute for Challenging Disorganization:
   www.challenging disorganization.org

✳ Plan for a New Life

Think for a moment about how your life is different now than before you began this program. We hope that you are spending less time acquiring, looking for lost items, or coping with clutter. We hope, too, that you have more opportunities and time to develop other activities and interests. If most of your time has been consumed by your things, you may have to make an effort to develop new activities. There is no shortage of fun and interesting things to do. We wish you well on your journey beyond hoarding.

Index

catastrophizing, 163, 172
categorization
    deciding on location for saved items,
        131–35
    making categories, 129–30
    overly elaborate, 46
    problems with, 69–70
change
    priority for, 35–39
    readiness for, 37–39, 102
charities that will pick up, 135–36
cheerleading, 62, 118
"churning," 150
clutter
    as magnet for clutter, 195–96
    reducing, 61
clutter visualization exercise, 99,
    159–60
coaches, instructions for, 62–63
cognitive-behavioral therapy
    (CBT), 7–8
compulsive acquiring process,
    110–12. *See also* acquiring
contract with self, 101
control
    beliefs about, 43, 181–82
    feelings of, 75–76
    solution, 108
coping
    developing alternative sources of,
        117–20
    with setbacks, 200–201
creative thinking, overly, 45–47, 72

daily activities impaired by hoarding.
    See Activities of Daily Living
    scale
decision-making
    following through with,
        150–51
    helping hoarders with, 62
    keep or let go, 148–50
    right to make own choices, 102
    problems with, 70
    taking over, 62, 63, 118. *See also*
        autonomy
    general plan for, 134, 134f
    questions for, 148–49
    skills, improving, 60

*Diagnostic and Statistical Manual of
    Mental Disorders* (DSM-5), 1,
    13–16, 23
Diogenes syndrome, 21
disorganization, chronic, 9
downward arrow strategy, 54–55, 164,
    172–75, 184

elderly, hoarding among, 22
emotional reasoning, 165
emotional support, providing, 62, 118
emotions
    hoarding-related, 73–76
    positive, 76
    (not) telling hoarders how they
        should feel, 63
    tolerating distress, 151. *See also*
        letting go of things
empathy, showing, 103
enjoyment, developing alternative
    sources of, 117–20
excuse making, 48–49

families, hoarding runs in, 18–19
family and friends, information and
    guidelines for, 4–5, 20, 62–63,
    92, 102–3, 118
feelings. *See* emotions
finding things, 60
focusing on present task, 62, 118

genetic component to hoarding, 18–19
goals, personal, 94–99. *See also* "bad
    guys"; hierarchy
    keeping your eyes on the prize, 159
guests, inviting to your home, 197

hauling, help with, 62
hierarchy, creating a non-acquiring,
    115–17
hierarchy form, 155
hoarding. *See also specific topics*
    defined, 14
    difficulty of getting control of
        one's, 2–3
    natural course of, 18–19
    readiness to work on, 91
    reasons to beat, 95–98
    recognizing, 88–91

resources on, 4–6, 201
severity, 16–18
special issues in, 19–22
strategies for beating, 53–61
synonyms and related terms, 2
understanding reasons for, 60
hoarding behavior, 76–78
Hoarding Disorder, 1, 13–16, 23
diagnostic criteria, 14–16
prevalence, 19
Hoarding of Animals Research
Consortium (HARC), 21, 22
Hoarding Rating Scale, 27–28, 30, 188
home
bringing others into, 197
photographs of, 34, 187–94
Home Environment Index (HEI),
32–34, 191–94
home safety, 29, 189–90
home visits from coaches, 62

identity
feelings of, 74–75
objects as a source of, 42, 178–80
insight, 19
poor/limited, 16, 92
Institute for Challenging
Disorganization, 9
International OCD Foundation, 4, 6

leisure. *See* enjoyment
letting go of things
advantages and disadvantages of,
168–70
experimenting with, 151–56
to keep or let go, 148–50, 168–70
rules for, 149–50, 196
life story, telling your, 91–93
limit setting, 104–5
living space, creating usable, 60
locating things. *See* finding things
locations
putting items in designated, 142–44
for saving, 131–35

medications, 9–10
memory
problems with, 70–71
underestimating, 42–43, 180–81

mental disorders. *See* psychiatric
disorders related to hoarding
mistakes, fear of making, 40, 171,
173–74
motivation boosters, 87, 99–100,
107–8, 121, 145–46
moving items, getting permission from
hoarders before, 63

neurobiology of hoarding, 66–71

obsessive-compulsive disorder
(OCD), 23
OHIO rule ("Only Handle It
Once"), 150
older people, hoarding among, 22
organizing (and sorting)
establishing a schedule for, 194–95
form to prepare for, 137–38
making rules for, 196
putting items in designated
locations, 142–44
strategies for, 129–35
over-creativity, 45–47, 72
overthinking, 45–47

paper (items)
filing
categories for, 139–40
items needed for, 140
how long to save, 141
special considerations for, 138–41
perceptions of self and others,
comparing, 88–91
perfectionism, 40–41, 72–73, 171
permission to touch or move items,
getting, 63
photographs of home
checking, 187–94
taking, 34
positive, discounting the, 163–64
positive feelings, 76
possessions. *See also specific topics*
attachment to, 41–42, 176–78
beliefs about usefulness of,
39–40, 167
beliefs about your, 39–45, 167–82
permission to touch or move, 63
as a source of identity, 42, 178–80